NATIONAL
GEOGRAPHIC
KiDS

DINOSAUR ATLAS

WHEN THEY ROAMED, HOW THEY LIVED, AND WHERE WE FIND THEIR FOSSILS

NATIONAL GEOGRAPHIC
WASHINGTON, D.C.

TABLE OF CONTENTS

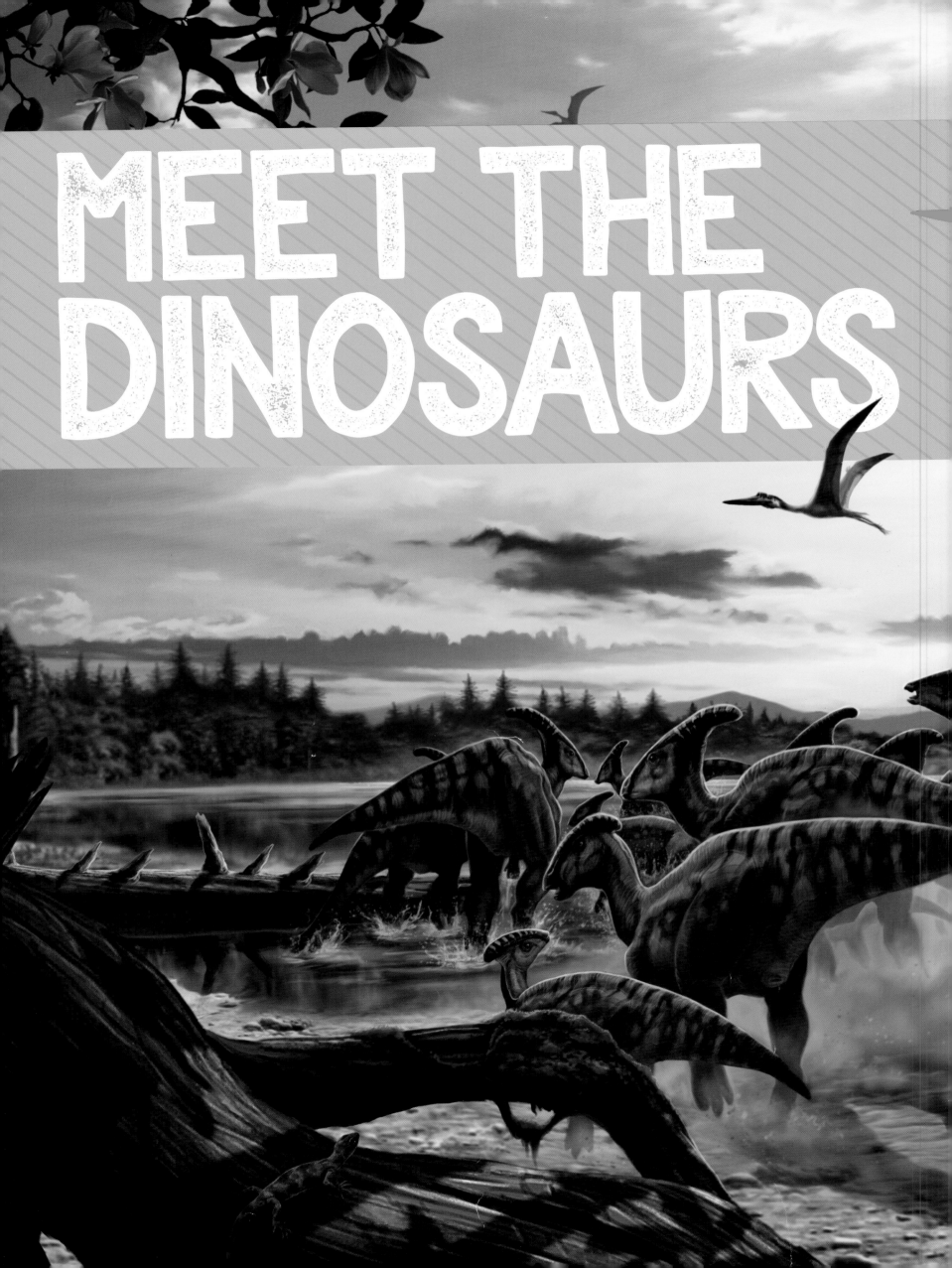

MEET THE DINOSAURS

THE WORLD BEFORE DINOSAURS

More than 250 million years ago (mya), our planet looked and felt a lot different from how it does today. Earth's climate was much more extreme. It was much hotter and more humid, and giant, flood-causing rainstorms called megamonsoons swept across the globe. The seven separate continents we have today hadn't yet taken shape. Instead, there was only one "supercontinent," called Pangaea. This period of time is known as the Permian period (299–252 mya).

During the Permian period, amphibians, early reptiles, and bony fish lived over the lands and in the seas. But then came the largest extinction event in the history of Earth. Around 90 percent of all the planet's species died. Scientists think it was caused by a chain of events that heated up the planet. The warmer climate changed what food was available for land and sea life. And without the right food, animals die. As the animals died, whole species became extinct. When a large number of species die out, it's called a mass extinction. Earth had lost most of its species, but this made way for the next period of time in history: the Mesozoic era, or the Age of Dinosaurs.

PREHISTORIC WORLD

PANTHALASSA (PANTHALASSIC OCEAN)

Late Permian (255 million years ago)

Equator

- Modern-day continents (see inset)
- Mountains
- Deep water
- Shallow water

0 — 2,000 miles
0 — 2,000 kilometers

PA

What Is a Paleontologist?

A paleontologist is a scientist who studies extinct animals, like dinosaurs, and the places they lived, known as habitats. These scientists study fossils, which are the remains or traces of something that was once alive. By studying fossils, paleontologists can learn how an animal moved, what it ate, or what the planet was like at the time the animal lived.

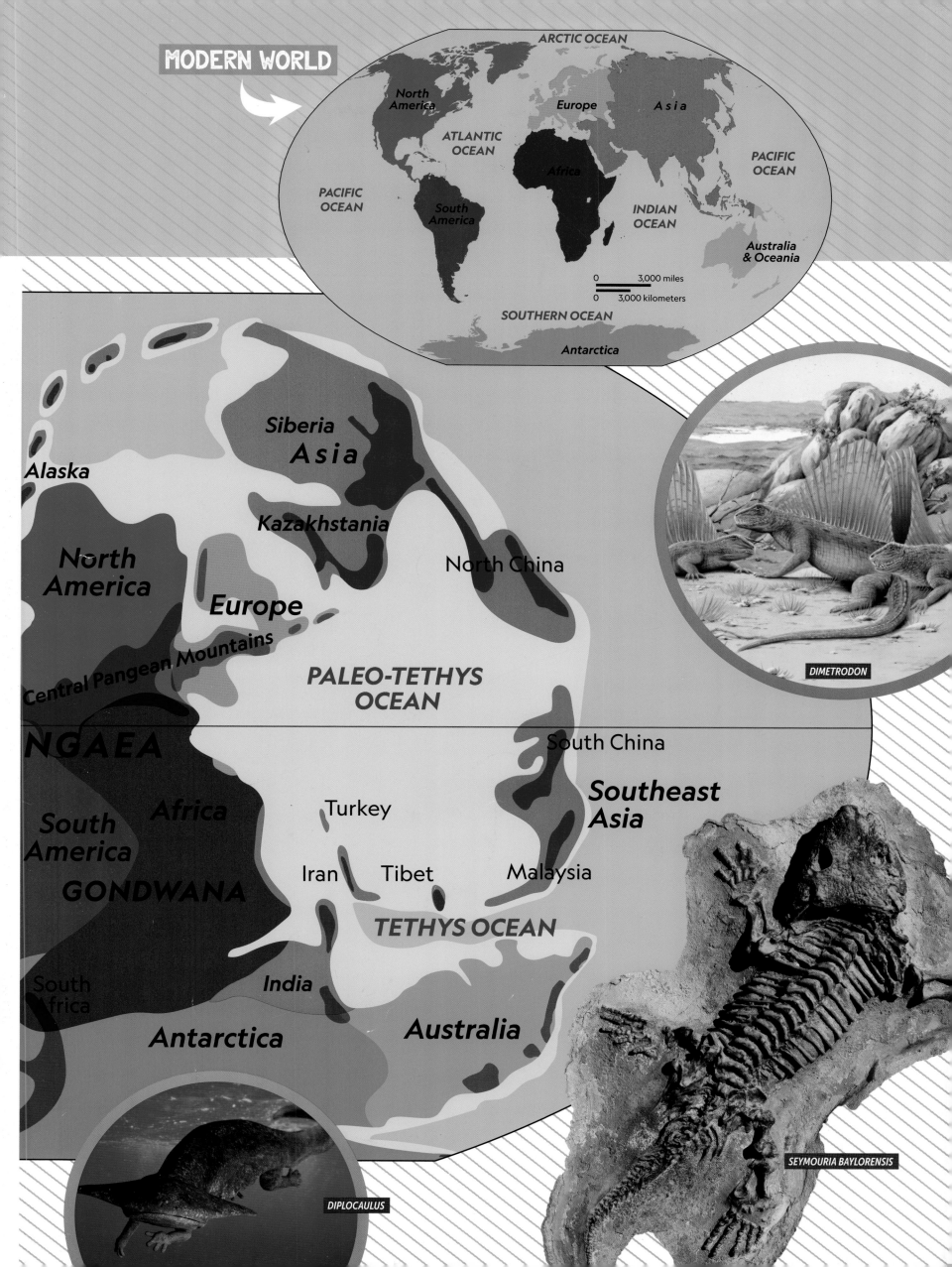

MODERN WORLD

ARCTIC OCEAN

North America

Europe

Asia

ATLANTIC OCEAN

PACIFIC OCEAN

Africa

PACIFIC OCEAN

South America

INDIAN OCEAN

Australia & Oceania

0   3,000 miles
0   3,000 kilometers

SOUTHERN OCEAN

Antarctica

Alaska

Siberia

Asia

Kazakhstania

North China

North America

Europe

Central Pangean Mountains

PALEO-TETHYS OCEAN

South China

PANGAEA

Southeast Asia

South America

Africa

Turkey

GONDWANA

Iran   Tibet   Malaysia

TETHYS OCEAN

South Africa

India

Antarctica

Australia

DIMETRODON

SEYMOURIA BAYLORENSIS

DIPLOCAULUS

WHEN DINOSAURS RULED THE EARTH

Scientists keep track of Earth's history by splitting it into different lengths of time. They base this on what was happening during those times. Scientists call the time before the dinosaurs the Paleozoic era (541–252 mya). They give the time after the mass extinction a different name: the Mesozoic era (252–66 mya). The time after the dinosaurs up to today is called the Cenozoic era (66 mya–present). Scientists also split each era up into smaller lengths of time, called periods. They split the Mesozoic era, the time of the dinosaurs, into three periods: the Triassic, the Jurassic, and the Cretaceous. No one knows for sure when dinosaurs first evolved, but scientists believe it was sometime during the Triassic period. During the Jurassic period, dinosaurs became common all over the world.

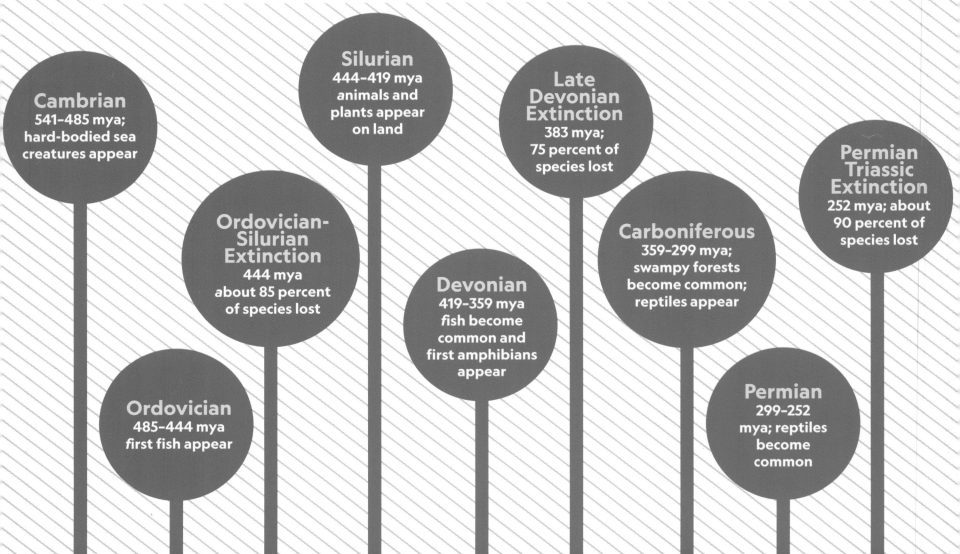

Cambrian
541–485 mya; hard-bodied sea creatures appear

Silurian
444–419 mya animals and plants appear on land

Late Devonian Extinction
383 mya; 75 percent of species lost

Permian Triassic Extinction
252 mya; about 90 percent of species lost

Ordovician-Silurian Extinction
444 mya about 85 percent of species lost

Carboniferous
359–299 mya; swampy forests become common; reptiles appear

Devonian
419–359 mya fish become common and first amphibians appear

Ordovician
485–444 mya first fish appear

Permian
299–252 mya; reptiles become common

PALEOZOIC
541–252 million years ago (mya)

OPABINIA REGALIS, A WATER ANIMAL FROM THE CAMBRIAN

HYNERIA, A DEVONIAN-PERIOD FISH

EDESTUS, A SHARK-LIKE CARBONIFEROUS-PERIOD FISH

Triassic
252–201 mya; crocodiles, ptero-saurs, dinosaurs, and mammals appear

Cretaceous-Paleogene Extinction
66 mya; about 75 percent of species lost

Cretaceous
145–66 mya; flowering plants become common

Neogene
23 mya–2.6 mya; earliest humans appear, mammal species spread

Triassic-Jurassic Extinction
201 mya; as much as 80 percent of species lost

Paleogene
66–23 mya; rodents, small horses, and elephants appear

Quaternary
2.6 mya–present; modern humans appear

Jurassic
201–145 mya; dinosaur giants and avian dinosaurs appear

MESOZOIC
252 to 66 mya

CENOZOIC
66 mya to present

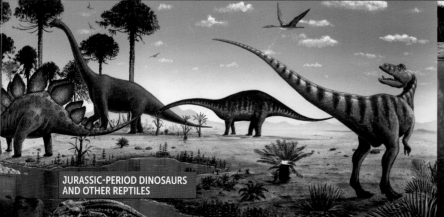

JURASSIC-PERIOD DINOSAURS AND OTHER REPTILES

CROCODYLUS THORBJARNARSONI, A NEOGENE-PERIOD REPTILE

MEGACEROPS, A NEOGENE-PERIOD MAMMAL

THE WORLD OF THE DINOSAURS

At the beginning of the Mesozoic era, the large supercontinent called Pangaea still existed. During the Jurassic period, it split into two different supercontinents: Laurasia in the north and Gondwana to the south. The splitting up of Pangaea happened because of something called tectonic shift. Earth's surface, or crust, is broken into large parts called plates. These plates are always moving. Over a really long period of time, the shifting plates caused parts of Pangaea to drift apart. The plates—and the continents—are still moving!

THE TRIASSIC PERIOD
ABOUT 252 MILLION TO 201 MILLION YEARS AGO

Scientists split the Triassic into three times: Early Triassic (about 252–247 mya), Middle Triassic (about 247–237 mya), and Late Triassic (about 237–201 mya).

At the start of the Triassic, all land on Earth was in one big supercontinent called Pangaea.

Near the end of this period, tectonic shift had broken the supercontinent in two.

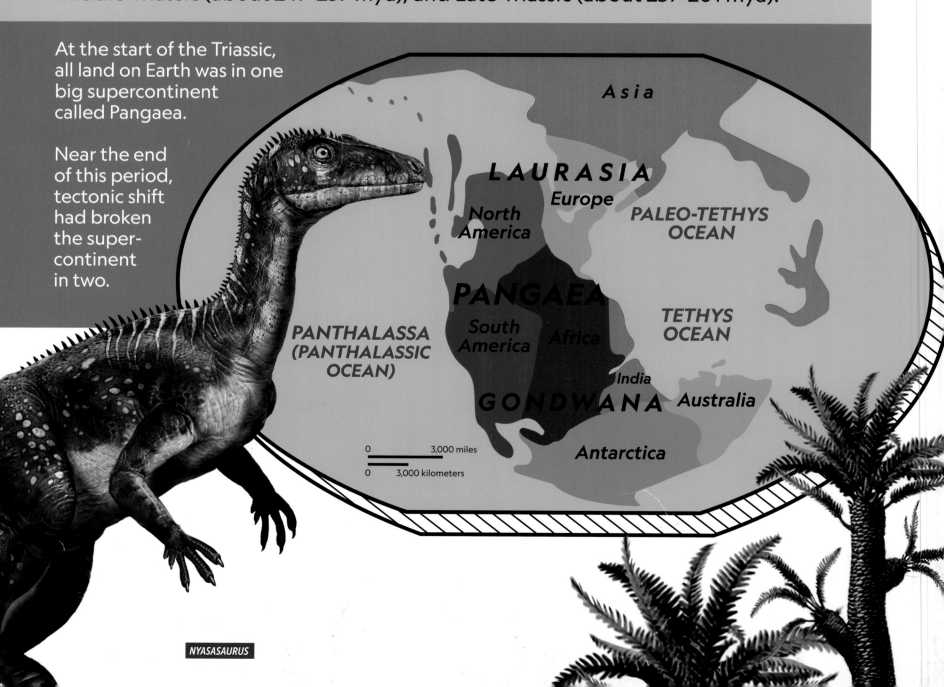

Asia

LAURASIA
Europe
North America
PALEO-TETHYS OCEAN

PANGAEA

PANTHALASSA (PANTHALASSIC OCEAN)
South America
Africa
TETHYS OCEAN

India
Australia

GONDWANA

Antarctica

0 ___ 3,000 miles
0 ___ 3,000 kilometers

NYASASAURUS

THE JURASSIC PERIOD
ABOUT 201 MILLION TO 145 MILLION YEARS AGO

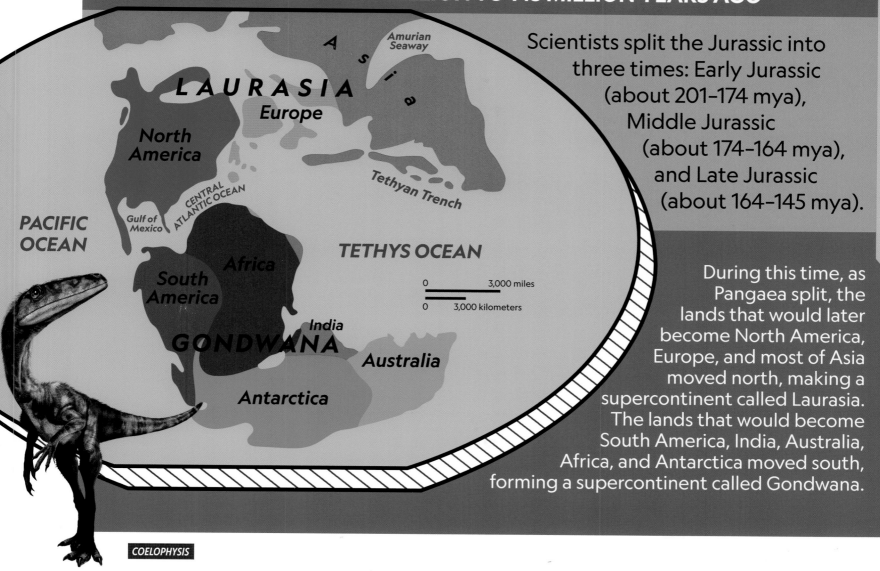

Scientists split the Jurassic into three times: Early Jurassic (about 201–174 mya), Middle Jurassic (about 174–164 mya), and Late Jurassic (about 164–145 mya).

During this time, as Pangaea split, the lands that would later become North America, Europe, and most of Asia moved north, making a supercontinent called Laurasia. The lands that would become South America, India, Australia, Africa, and Antarctica moved south, forming a supercontinent called Gondwana.

COELOPHYSIS

THE CRETACEOUS PERIOD
ABOUT 145 MILLION TO 66 MILLION YEARS AGO

Scientists split the Cretaceous period into two times: Early Cretaceous (about 145–101 mya) and Late Cretaceous (about 101–66 mya).

During this time, the land continued breaking and moving into the continents we know today. But they were in slightly different spots. For example, India had broken away from Africa and was moving slowly toward Asia.

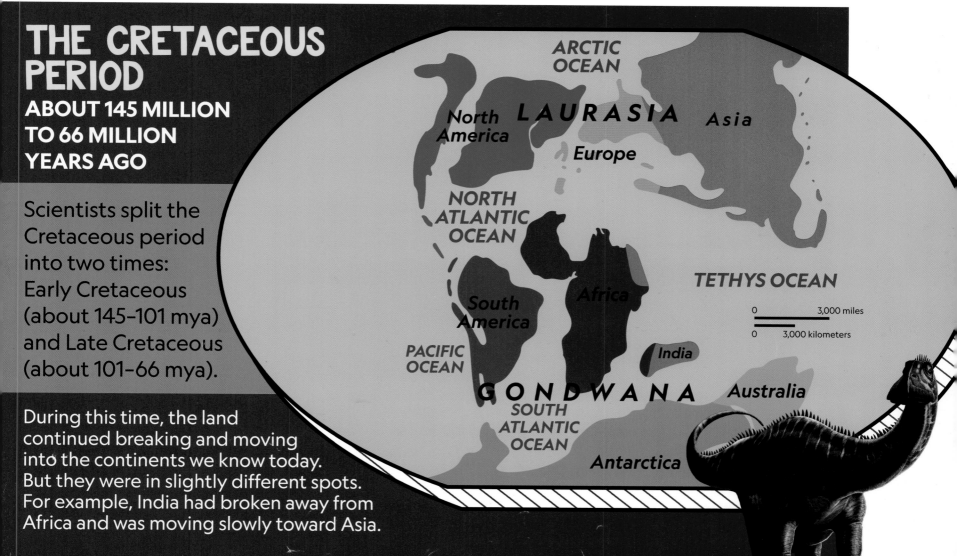

NIGERSAURUS

WHAT IS A DINOSAUR?

When you picture a dinosaur, what do you see? A towering *T. rex*? An armored *Ankylosaurus*? A sail-backed *Spinosaurus*? Dinosaurs came in all shapes and sizes. Some were as small as a dog. Others were as big as a house. They could eat plants or meat—or both! They had scales, feathers, or armor. Some ran on two legs, and some walked on four.

So, what made a dinosaur a dinosaur? Dinosaurs evolved from small reptiles during the Triassic period. Besides dinosaurs, the reptile group has included lizards, snakes, turtles, crocodiles, and birds (p. 112). Throughout time, most reptiles have laid hard-shelled eggs on land. They have had scales, armored skin, or feathers. But dinosaurs had a type of hip bone that other reptiles haven't had. This special hip bone allowed dinosaurs to stand with their legs right under their bodies. Other early reptiles had bowed-out legs, like crocodiles.

In 1842, British scientist Sir Richard Owen came up with the word "Dinosauria" after studying reptile fossils that were different from anything he'd seen before. It comes from two Greek words and can be translated as "terrible lizard."

DINOSAUR BONE UNDER THE MICROSCOPE

HOW OLD IS THAT DINOSAUR?

Paleontologists can tell how old a fossil is by looking at the rock the fossil is in. If they figure out how old the rock is, that tells them about how old the fossil is. But how can they tell what age the dinosaur was when it died? The answer is partially found in something called concentric rings (also known as growth rings). Concentric rings are two or more circles with the same center point. If you slice a fossilized dinosaur bone in half and look at it under a microscope, you'll find concentric circles. These are just like what you would find in the trunk of a tree. For dinosaurs, each circle you see means one year of age.

OTHER AMAZING REPTILES

Dinosaurs were reptiles, but not all prehistoric reptiles were dinosaurs. Giant marine reptiles like plesiosaurs and ichthyosaurs (p. 29) swam through the ocean during the time of dinosaurs. Prehistoric reptiles took to the skies, too. These flying creatures were called pterosaurs, which means "winged lizard."

QUETZALCOATLUS,
A PTEROSAUR

SHONISAURUS,
AN ICHTHYOSAUR

TYRANNOSAURUS

Scientists give dinosaurs two names: a genus and a species. A genus is a larger group that has several species in it. All life on Earth is grouped in this way. For example, humans (or *Homo sapiens*) are the species *sapiens* of a genus called *Homo*. Sometimes, scientists know the genus of a fossil but not the exact species.

DINO FAMILY TREE

When dinosaurs first appeared during the Triassic period, they were two-legged, meat-eating reptiles. These first dinosaurs lived on Pangaea and were all very similar. But after the continents began to break apart, different kinds of habitats formed in different places. The lands started to change. And dinosaurs started to change, too. Soon the dinosaurs in one place started to look different from dinosaurs that lived in other places.

When scientists began to study dinosaurs in the 1800s, they noticed that many dinosaurs looked different from each other. The scientists wanted a way to sort the dinosaurs into different categories. They split them into two groups based on the shapes of the dinosaurs' hip bones. All dinosaurs have three hip bones on each side. But the front bone, known as the pubis, pointed forward for some dinosaurs and backward for others. The scientists called the dinosaurs with forward-pointing pubis bones saurischians, meaning "lizard-hipped." They called the dinosaurs with backward-pointing pubis bones ornithischians, meaning "bird-hipped."

Since then, scientists have sorted dinosaurs into even more categories based on the way that dinosaurs evolved over millions of years. Take a look at the dinosaur family tree to see how some of the many types of dinosaurs are related!

HETERODONTOSAURS

DINOSAURIA

ORNITHISCHIANS
Bird-hipped dinosaurs

SAUROPODS

SAUROPODOMORPHS

SAURISCHIANS
Lizard-hipped dinosaurs

THEROPODS

WHAT'S IN A NAME?

Dinosaur names often come from two ancient languages: ancient Greek or Latin. They usually describe how the dinosaurs looked or acted.

Allosaur
"Strange lizard"

Ceratopsian
"Horn-faced"

Maniraptoran
"Hand thief"

Ankylosaur
"Joined-bone lizard"

Hadrosaur
"Bulk lizard"

Megalosaur
"Big lizard"

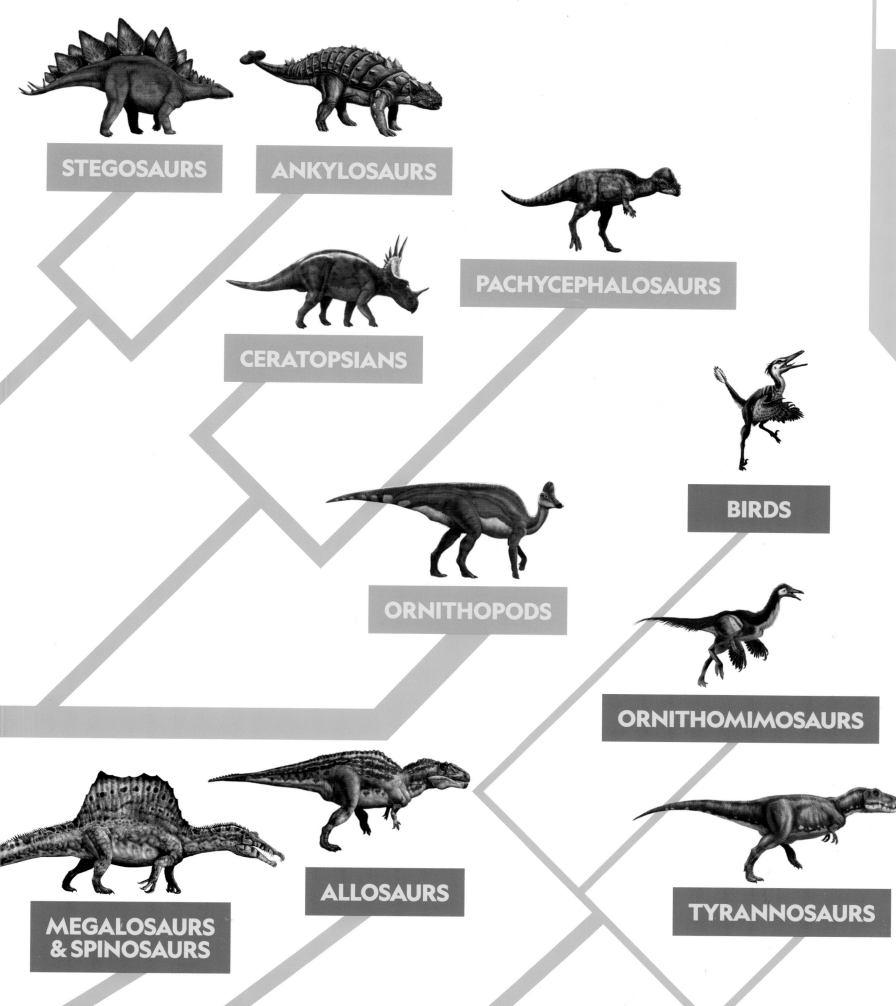

STEGOSAURS

ANKYLOSAURS

PACHYCEPHALOSAURS

CERATOPSIANS

BIRDS

ORNITHOPODS

ORNITHOMIMOSAURS

MEGALOSAURS & SPINOSAURS

ALLOSAURS

TYRANNOSAURS

Ornithomimosaur	Pachycephalosaur	Spinosaur	Titanosaur	Thyreophoran
"Bird-copying lizard"	"Thick-headed lizard"	"Spine lizard"	"Giant lizard"	"Shield carrier"
Ornithopod	**Sauropod**	**Stegosaur**	**Theropod**	**Tyrannosaur**
"Bird-footed"	"Lizard-footed"	"Roof lizard"	"Beast-footed"	"Tyrant lizard"

ALL ABOUT FOSSILS

Fossils are the remains or traces of animals and plants that lived long ago. Animal bones are some of the best known fossils, but leaves, shells, and feathers can also become fossilized. Some fossils are made from a mix of minerals and a living thing's hard parts, like bones, teeth, or horns. Other fossils are the things an animal left behind, like footprints, poop, and even vomit!

Scientists study fossils to learn what dinosaurs looked like and what they ate. They can also learn how dinosaurs behaved and what the planet was like while dinosaurs were alive. Fossils can't tell us everything. But without fossils, we wouldn't know anything about dinosaurs! Luckily, there are many kinds of fossils to study.

Body Fossils

Body fossils are the bits of the hard parts left behind after an animal or plant dies. These parts, like bones or teeth, mix with minerals in the environment over long periods of time. For a body fossil to form, an animal has to be quickly covered with mud or sand right before or after it dies. As thousands of years pass, the mud or sand turns to rock. The animal's soft body parts rot. Then minerals slowly flow into the leftover hard body parts. This mix of mineral and hard bits hardens, eventually turning into a fossil.

Some fossils are called petrified. Petrified means that something has been changed into stone. When people think of petrified fossils, they usually think of petrified wood—the fossils of ancient trees. These fossils are made the same way that skeletons become fossils. A tree's material is replaced by minerals. Petrified Forest National Park in Arizona, U.S.A., is filled with petrified trees. They look like glittering crystals because they have turned into a sparkling mineral called quartz.

DINO DISCOVERER: Lisa White

All living things can make a fossil in the right setting. But what if the plants and animals are too tiny to see? They form microfossils! Lisa White is an American scientist. She's a micropaleontologist. This means that she studies microfossils that are much too small for humans to see with their eyes alone. White uses a microscope to search rocks and sediment for the fossils of teeny ocean plants called plankton. While they may not seem like much, these plankton microfossils can tell White a lot about what Earth was like hundreds of millions of years ago.

Molds and Casts

If you press a seashell into soft wet sand and then remove it, you will see a mark in the shape of the shell left behind. Now imagine if that soft sand hardened into rock over thousands of years. It would create a mold: a hardened version of the mark the seashell left. Then, more rock materials could fill the mold and harden, which creates a copy of the shell, also called a cast. These molds and casts are both types of fossils. They help scientists today learn about plants and ocean life from the past.

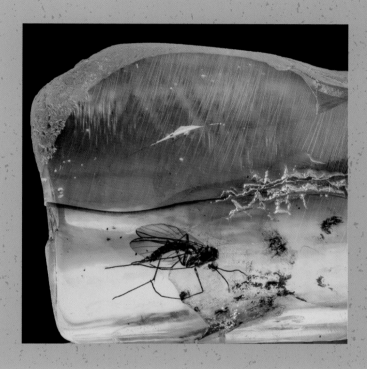

Amber

Some fossils are trapped in amber. Amber is resin, a goo that oozes from some trees, that has hardened over a long time. As sticky resin leaks out and drips down a tree, insects, plants, and animal parts like feathers can get stuck inside it. The resin hardens and—over millions of years—turns into amber. Anything trapped inside amber is preserved, and it is kept almost perfectly in its original state.

Trace Fossils

A dinosaur footprint is a perfect example of a trace fossil: It is not a fossil of the animal itself, but of something the animal left behind. Trackways are fossils of several footprints found together. They can help scientists learn how dinosaurs moved and if they spent time together or alone.

Trace fossils also include coprolites, which are fossilized poop, and gastric pellets, which are fossilized vomit. Scientists can study fossilized poop and vomit to determine what a dinosaur ate. One group of scientists found rotting wood and small pieces of crustacean shells inside fossilized dinosaur poop. This told them the dinosaur may have been searching for insects that lived in wood. It also told them the dinosaur lived near an ocean, because that's where most crustaceans are found.

PREHISTORIC PLANET

TRIASSIC PERIOD

252 MILLION–201 MILLION YEARS AGO

At the end of the Permian period, there was a giant mass extinction known as the Great Dying. Much life on Earth disappeared, but reptiles were one kind of animal to survive. Soon, life on Earth began to return, and new animals and plants appeared on land and in the sea. Scientists think of this time—about 252 million years ago—as the start of the Triassic period.

During the Triassic period, reptiles evolved in new ways. Scientists call this group of Triassic reptiles archosaurs. Archosaurs include many kinds of crocodiles of different shapes and sizes. This group also includes birds and extinct flying reptiles like pterosaurs. And it includes the first dinosaurs. Unlike many dinosaurs that evolved later, the first dinosaurs were small creatures that ran on two legs. Other animals evolved too, including the first mammals.

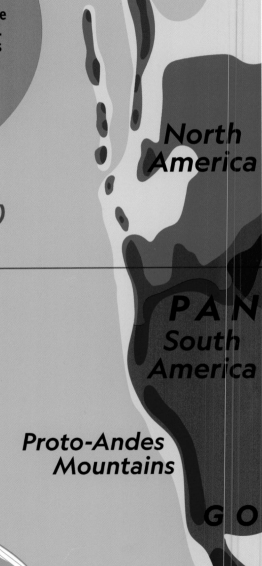

The east coast of modern-day South America and the west coast of Africa fit together like two pieces of a puzzle. That's because they were once joined as part of Pangaea. The layers of rock in Scotland's Caledonian Mountains and the Appalachian Mountains of the East Coast of the United States are also related.

PANTHALASSA (PANTHALASSIC OCEAN)

Late Triassic (237 million years ago)

- Mountains
- Deep water
- Shallow water

0 — 2,000 miles
0 — 2,000 kilometers

North America

PAN

South America

Proto-Andes Mountains

GO

How Do Fossils Prove Pangaea Existed?

Svalbard, a group of islands in Norway, is a very cold place today. But fossils of tropical plants have been found there. These fossils helped scientist Alfred Wegener realize that what is now the Arctic had once been hot and humid. Otherwise, those tropical plants couldn't have survived! Wegener helped come up with the theory that all the continents had once been part of a supercontinent. He called it Pangaea, which means "all the Earth." Wegener believed that Pangaea had broken into pieces that drifted away from each other. Further evidence has shown he was right!

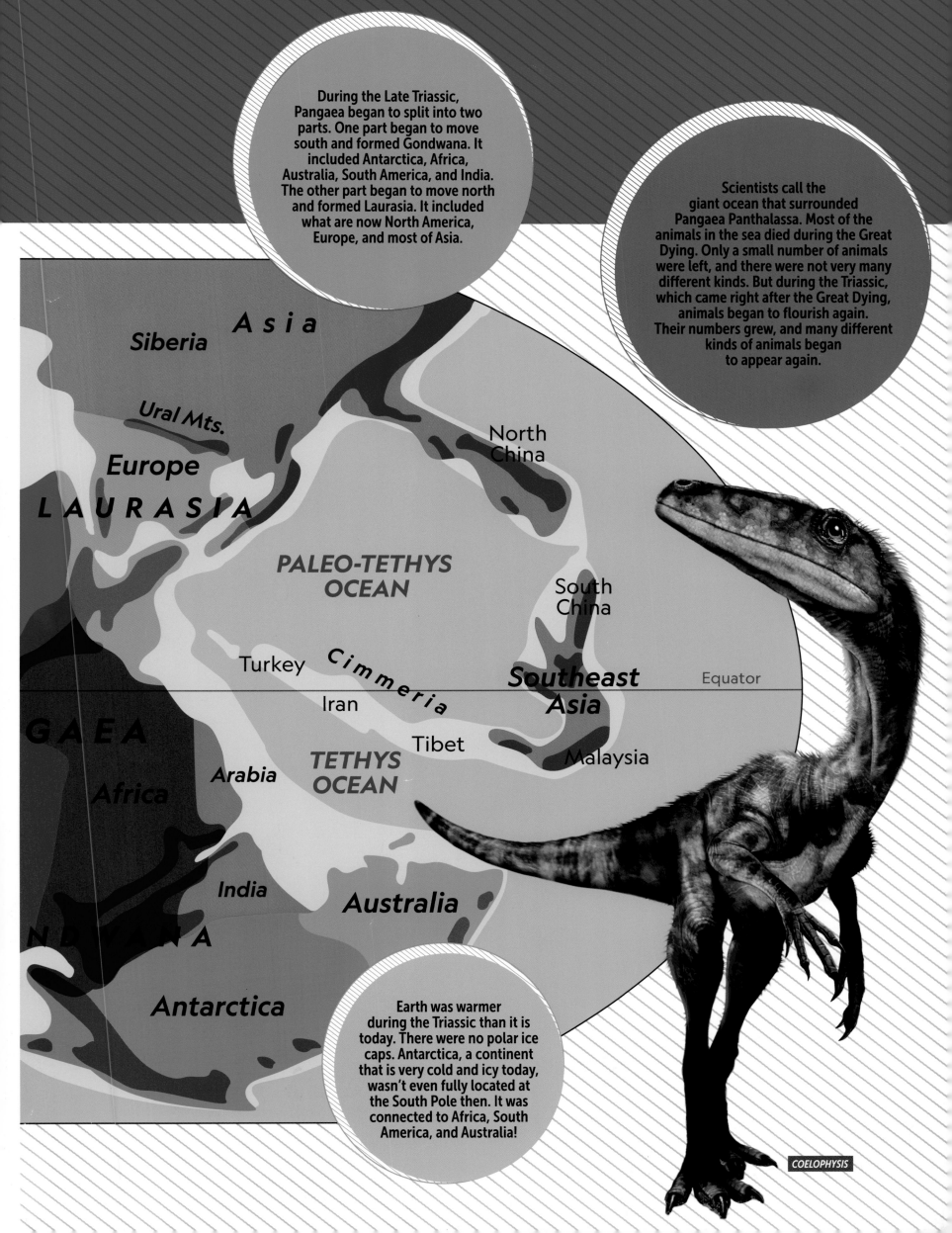

During the Late Triassic, Pangaea began to split into two parts. One part began to move south and formed Gondwana. It included Antarctica, Africa, Australia, South America, and India. The other part began to move north and formed Laurasia. It included what are now North America, Europe, and most of Asia.

Scientists call the giant ocean that surrounded Pangaea Panthalassa. Most of the animals in the sea died during the Great Dying. Only a small number of animals were left, and there were not very many different kinds. But during the Triassic, which came right after the Great Dying, animals began to flourish again. Their numbers grew, and many different kinds of animals began to appear again.

Earth was warmer during the Triassic than it is today. There were no polar ice caps. Antarctica, a continent that is very cold and icy today, wasn't even fully located at the South Pole then. It was connected to Africa, South America, and Australia!

A s i a

Siberia

Ural Mts.

Europe

LAURASIA

North China

PALEO-TETHYS OCEAN

South China

Turkey

C i m m e r i a

Southeast Asia

Equator

Iran

GAEA

Tibet

Malaysia

Africa

Arabia

TETHYS OCEAN

India

Australia

NDWANA

Antarctica

COELOPHYSIS

TRIASSIC HABITATS

Because Pangaea was so huge, its climate was very different from place to place. The supercontinent was at Earth's Equator, so much of the continent was hot.

The Land

Coastal areas were filled with green plants like mosses and ferns. Many trees, including pines, redwoods, ginkgoes, and cycads—which looked like miniature palm trees— grew there, too. Farther inland, there were wide open plains and deserts.

While all of these plants and animals lived during this time, they would not likely have lived in the same place or even at the exact same time.

The Air

Because Pangaea was a supercontinent, the land in its center was far from ocean water. This central area received little rain and had little moisture in the air. This led to a hot, dry, desert-like climate. But the ocean water along the coastlines caused rainy seasons that brought a lot of rain. That meant plants could grow.

The Water

The Panthalassa Ocean surrounded Pangaea. During the Great Dying, chemicals and high temperatures had made the ocean a place where it was hard for animals to live. But as it recovered, it burst with new life. Corals had survived the extinction and began to grow in new ways. So did certain microscopic algae and bacteria, called phytoplankton, that sea creatures could eat. Then many new marine animals appeared, including ancient squid and porpoise-like ichthyosaurs (p. 29).

TRIASSIC DINOSAURS

The Triassic period is often called "The Dawn of the Dinosaurs." That's because dinosaurs first appeared around the Late Triassic. At their beginning, dinosaurs weren't at the top of the food chain. They definitely did not rule Earth yet! They were small, ranging from the size of a cat to the size of a pony. There also weren't very many of them.

EORAPTOR
(EE-oh-RAP-tor)

MEANING: "Early thief"

PERIOD: Late Triassic

LOCATION: Argentina

Eoraptor was one of the earliest dinosaurs, but it wasn't discovered until 1991. It was no bigger than a fox. It had razor-sharp teeth that curved backward—perfect for eating meat.

More Triassic Dinosaurs

Chindesaurus
(CHIN-dee-SORE-us):
"Chinde lizard,"
U.S.A., Late Triassic

Liliensternus
(lil-ee-en-SHTERN-us):
Named for Count Hugo Rühle
von Lilienstern, France and
Germany, Late Triassic

Herrerasaurus
(herr-ray-rah-SORE-us):
"Herrera's lizard,"
Argentina, Late Triassic

COELOPHYSIS
(SEE-low-FY-sis)

MEANING: "Hollow form"

PERIOD: Late Triassic to Early Jurassic

LOCATION: Southwestern United States; South Africa; Zimbabwe

Coelophysis was named for the hollow bones in its arms and legs. These hollow bones likely made this two-legged dinosaur fast, letting it quickly catch meals.

RIOJASAURUS
(ree-OH-hah-SORE-us)

MEANING: "Lizard from La Rioja"

PERIOD: Late Triassic

LOCATION: Argentina

This long-necked prosauropod, or early plant-eating dinosaur, walked on four legs. That's unusual because most dinosaurs at this time walked on two legs.

Procompsognathus
(PRO-COMP-sog-NAY-thus):
"Before the elegant jaw,"
Germany, Late Triassic

Guaibasaurus
(GWIE-bah-SORE-us): "[Rio] Guaiba lizard," Brazil, Late Triassic

Thecodontosaurus
(THEEK-o-DON-toh-SORE-us):
"Socket-toothed lizard,"
United Kingdom,
Late Triassic

TRIASSIC LIFE

Many other interesting creatures lived on land and in the sea during the Triassic period. Sea urchins, which are spiny round creatures, thrived in Triassic waters. So did mollusks, like snails, squid, and oysters. Centipedes, millipedes, and scorpions ran across the ground. Grasshoppers appeared during this time. Larger reptiles, like phytosaurs, ruled on land. But unlike dinosaurs, they wouldn't survive past the Triassic.

Placerias

(pluh-SEHR-ree-us) Late Triassic

This reptile was a far-off relative of mammals. It looked like a hippopotamus with a pointed beak and downward-pointing tusks. It used those tusks to dig for roots. It also ate other parts of plants.

Cynodont

**(SIE-noh-dahnt)
Late Triassic through
Early Jurassic**

This small, warm-blooded reptile looked like a scaly rat with pointy teeth. It lived in underground homes called burrows. All mammals evolved from cynodonts—including humans!

Phytosaur

(FY-toe-sore) Late Triassic

These scaled reptiles had long jaws filled with sharp teeth. They could snap at anything that came near them—even dinosaurs. They looked like modern crocodiles, but their nostrils were near their eyes instead of at the end of their snouts.

Ichthyosaur
(ick-THEE-oh-sore)
Late Triassic through
Late Cretaceous

The ichthyosaur, or "fish lizard," lived through the entire Mesozoic era. This marine reptile was most common during the Triassic and Jurassic periods. It had a long, lizard-like body and fins. Scientists think it could move at speeds of more than 22 miles an hour (35.4 km/h)—as fast as a car on a neighborhood street.

Eozostrodon
(EE-oh-ZO-struh-don) Late Triassic

Thought to be one of the earliest mammals, this shrew-like creature was three feet (0.9 m) long. It laid eggs and nursed its babies with milk.

Aetosaur (AY-toe-sore) Late Triassic

The aetosaur had a crocodile-like body, a triangle-shaped head, a pointed snout, and protective body armor. This reptile could grow to be 10 feet (3 m) long. It ate mostly plants.

JURASSIC PERIOD
201 MILLION–145 MILLION YEARS AGO

At the end of the Triassic period, there was another mass extinction. Scientists believe it was caused by volcanic eruptions that spewed out gases that raised temperatures and made it hard for many animals to breathe or eat. Dinosaurs survived this extinction. They continued to grow in number—and size. Huge dinosaurs, such as long-necked sauropods like the *Apatosaurus*, came to be during the Jurassic period. *Archaeopteryx* (p. 75), which may have been one of the planet's first avian dinosaurs, took to the skies. Ichthyosaurs, giant crocodiles, and plesiosaurs continued to swim the seas. Tropical weather brought more plants, which giant-size dinosaurs ate to survive. Dinosaurs were now common all over Earth.

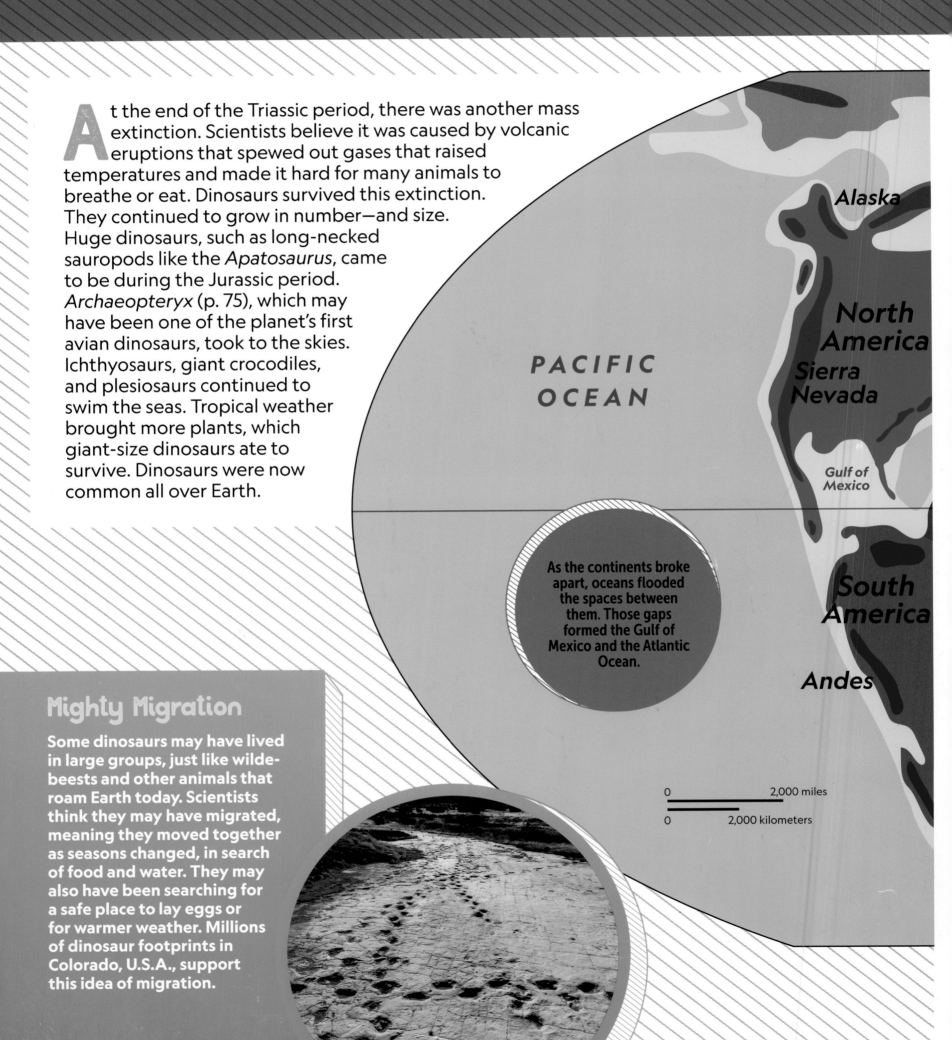

PACIFIC OCEAN

Alaska

North America

Sierra Nevada

Gulf of Mexico

South America

Andes

As the continents broke apart, oceans flooded the spaces between them. Those gaps formed the Gulf of Mexico and the Atlantic Ocean.

0 ——— 2,000 miles

0 ——— 2,000 kilometers

Mighty Migration

Some dinosaurs may have lived in large groups, just like wildebeests and other animals that roam Earth today. Scientists think they may have migrated, meaning they moved together as seasons changed, in search of food and water. They may also have been searching for a safe place to lay eggs or for warmer weather. Millions of dinosaur footprints in Colorado, U.S.A., support this idea of migration.

During the Jurassic period, Gondwana began to split. Africa and South America moved west. India, Antarctica, Madagascar, and Australia moved east.

The continents continued to break apart during the Jurassic period. New species of animals and plants appeared on these different land areas. Because these living things were separated by huge distances and living in different habitats, they changed in different ways.

Avian dinosaurs were reptiles that had feathers and could mostly fly. Modern birds are avian dinosaurs that survived extinction (p. 112).

Siberia

Amurian Seaway

A s i a

Ural Mts.

North China

LAURASIA

Europe

South China

Iran

Tibet

Turkey

Tethyan Trench

Southeast Asia

CENTRAL ATLANTIC OCEAN

TETHYS OCEAN

Late Jurassic (152 million years ago)

Equator

Arabia

Africa

Mountains

Deep water

Shallow water

Madagascar

India

GONDWANA

Australia

Antarctica

ARCHAEOPTERYX

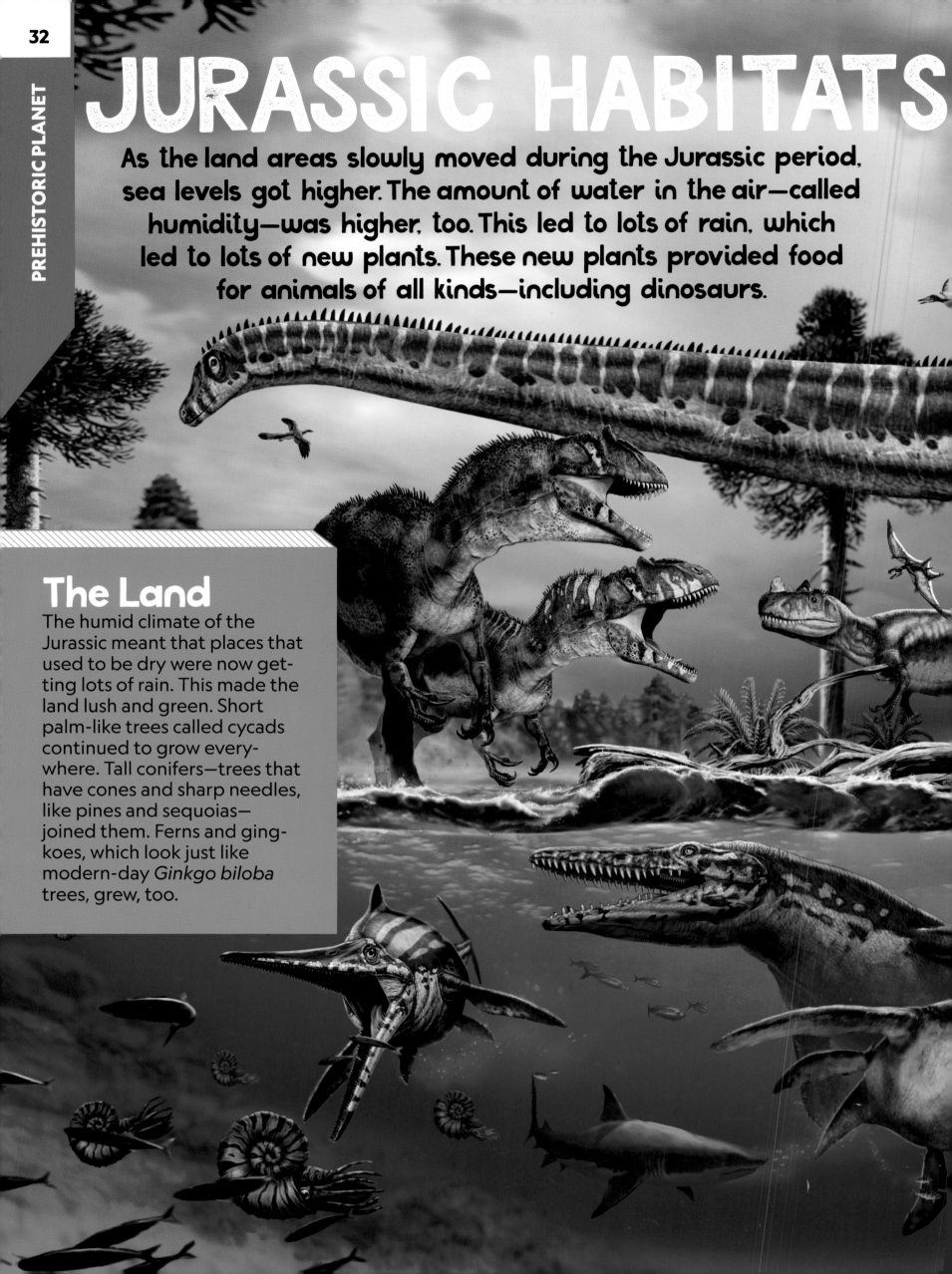

JURASSIC HABITATS

As the land areas slowly moved during the Jurassic period, sea levels got higher. The amount of water in the air—called humidity—was higher, too. This led to lots of rain, which led to lots of new plants. These new plants provided food for animals of all kinds—including dinosaurs.

The Land

The humid climate of the Jurassic meant that places that used to be dry were now getting lots of rain. This made the land lush and green. Short palm-like trees called cycads continued to grow everywhere. Tall conifers—trees that have cones and sharp needles, like pines and sequoias— joined them. Ferns and gingkoes, which look just like modern-day *Ginkgo biloba* trees, grew, too.

The Air

Summers were now hot and humid with lots of rainfall. Winters were mild. Temperatures were cooler than they had been during the Triassic period. But it was still warmer than it is today.

The Water

The ocean continued to burst with new life. Because the land areas continued to break apart, there were more coastlines. This meant there were more shallow places for ocean animals to live. There were giant marine crocodiles, sharks, rays, and relatives of the modern squid. There were also more ichthyosaurs and plesiosaurs. Even away from the coasts, some bodies of water—like the seas of central Laurasia—were warm and shallow.

While all of these plants and animals lived during this time, they would not likely have lived in the same place or even at the exact same time.

JURASSIC DINOSAURS

During this 56-million-year period, dinosaurs—especially sauropods—ruled the Earth. Sauropods were the biggest dinosaurs. In fact, they were the largest land animals ever! Many different kinds of sauropods began to appear during the middle of the Jurassic. Their fossils have been found on every continent. Other types of dinosaurs lived during the Jurassic, too, such as armored dinosaurs and flesh-eating theropods.

STEGOSAURUS
(STEG-oh-SORE-us)

MEANING:
"Roof lizard"

PERIOD:
Late Jurassic

LOCATION: U.S.A.

Stegosaurus had plates on its back and spikes on its tail. This plant-eater was slow moving. But its powerful spiked tail could be used as a weapon against predators like *Allosaurus* and *Ceratosaurus*.

More Jurassic Dinosaurs

Brachiosaurus
(BRAK-ee-oh-SORE-us):
"Arm lizard,"
U.S.A., Late Jurassic

Camptosaurus
(KAMP-toe-SORE-us):
"Bent lizard,"
United Kingdom,
U.S.A., Late Jurassic

Ornitholestes
(OR-nith-oh-LES-teez):
"Bird robber,"
U.S.A., Late Jurassic

ALLOSAURUS
(AL-oh-SORE-us)

MEANING: "Strange lizard"

PERIOD: Late Jurassic

LOCATION: Portugal; U.S.A.

This deadly carnivore was 28 feet (8.5 m) long. About 70 sharp teeth curved backward to keep prey from escaping its mouth. Its lower jawbones bent outward, which made extra room in its mouth for holding on to its dinner.

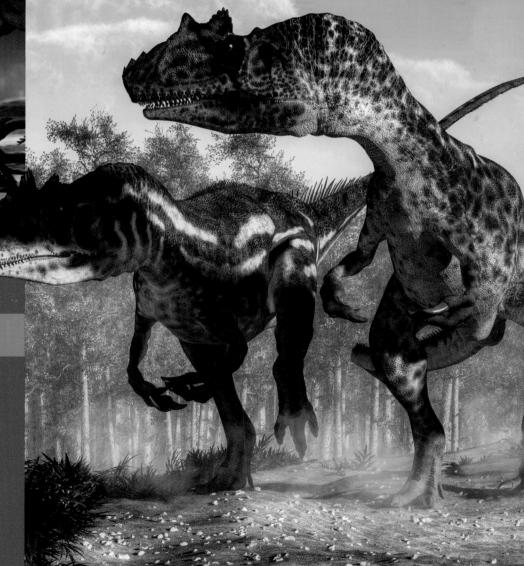

APATOSAURUS
(uh-PAT-uh-SORE-us)

MEANING: "Tricky lizard"

PERIOD: LATE JURASSIC

LOCATION: U.S.A.

The giant-size *Apatosaurus* could grow to be about 70 feet (21.3 m) long—that's almost as long as two city buses. Its legs were thick like an elephant's. Its long, flexible neck let it eat from the tallest forest trees.

Megalosaurus
(MEG-ah-low-SORE-us):
"Big lizard,"
United Kingdom,
Middle Jurassic

Juravenator
(ju-RAH-ve-NAY-tor): "Hunter from Jura," Germany, Late Jurassic

Diplodocus
(DIP-low-DOCK-us):
"Double beam,"
U.S.A., Late Jurassic

JURASSIC LIFE

There were many different kinds of animals on Earth during the Jurassic. Small mammals ran around the feet of dinosaurs. Life thrived in the warm ocean waters, including rays, sharks, snails and mollusks, sea urchins, and sea stars, just to name a few. Pterosaurs and insects flew about the green lands and warm skies of the Jurassic period.

Excalibosaurus
(ex-CAL-ih-bo-SORE-us) Early Jurassic

A type of ichthyosaur, *Excalibosaurus* was named for its unusual jaw. Because its upper mouth (also called the rostrum) stuck out far over its lower jaw, the *Excalibosaurus* looked a bit like the swordfish of today. Its name comes from a famous legendary sword, Excalibur.

Belemnite
(BELL-em-nite)
Paleozoic era to
Late Cretaceous period

Though this squid-like marine animal may have first appeared more than 360 million years ago, it became common during the Jurassic and Cretaceous periods. It had a long shell that ended in what looked like a parrot's beak and 10 arms with hooks to catch prey like small fish and crustaceans.

Hadrocodium
(had-row-CODE-ee-um)
Early Jurassic

The furry *Hadrocodium*, one of the tiniest Mesozoic animals, was only two inches (5 cm) long. But this mammal had a huge brain for a little creature. Its brain was about 50 percent bigger than brains of other early mammals when compared to their body size.

Flying Insects
Devonian through today

Insects have been around since well before the Jurassic or even Triassic period. The Devonian period, when they first appeared, was more than 400 million years ago. Later, during the Carboniferous period, they reached huge sizes—some insects similar to dragonflies had wingspans more than two feet (0.6 m) wide! But by the end of the Jurassic, they had shrunk by a lot. Some scientists think this is because avian dinosaurs were now around. Being smaller would have let insects escape flying predators more easily.

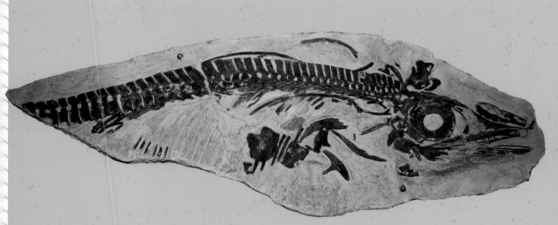

Ophthalmosaurus
(OP-thal-moh-SORE-us)
Middle Jurassic to Late Jurassic

Ophthalmosaurus, a type of ichthyosaur, had the largest eyes of any animal that has ever existed. Its eyes were bigger than soccer balls! Scientists believe the large eyes helped it catch squid and small fish in dark, deep waters.

Juramaia
(JUR-uh-MYE-uh) Late Jurassic

Juramaia was a small mammal similar to a shrew. Its paws let it climb trees easily, where it likely hunted for insects. This small rodent-like critter is one of the earliest close cousins of all "placental animals," or animals that give birth to almost fully formed babies instead of laying eggs—like humans!

Cricosaurus
(CREE-co-SORE-us) Late Jurassic

Crocodiles first appeared during the Late Triassic period. During the Jurassic, they began to grow larger. *Cricosaurus* had paddle-like limbs and a tail fin like today's dolphins. This reptile also had long, powerful jaws like modern-day crocodiles.

CRETACEOUS PERIOD

145 MILLION–66 MILLION YEARS AGO

The Cretaceous was the last and longest period of the Mesozoic era. Many animals and plants of the Jurassic period were still around. Pterosaurs still flew through the skies. Plesiosaurs and other marine reptiles still swam in the oceans. Dinosaurs of all shapes and sizes walked the land, including a new dinosaur: *Tyrannosaurus rex*. Land areas continued to break apart, and life on Earth continued to change. And by the end of this period, all dinosaurs except for birds—and about 75 percent of the species on Earth—would become extinct.

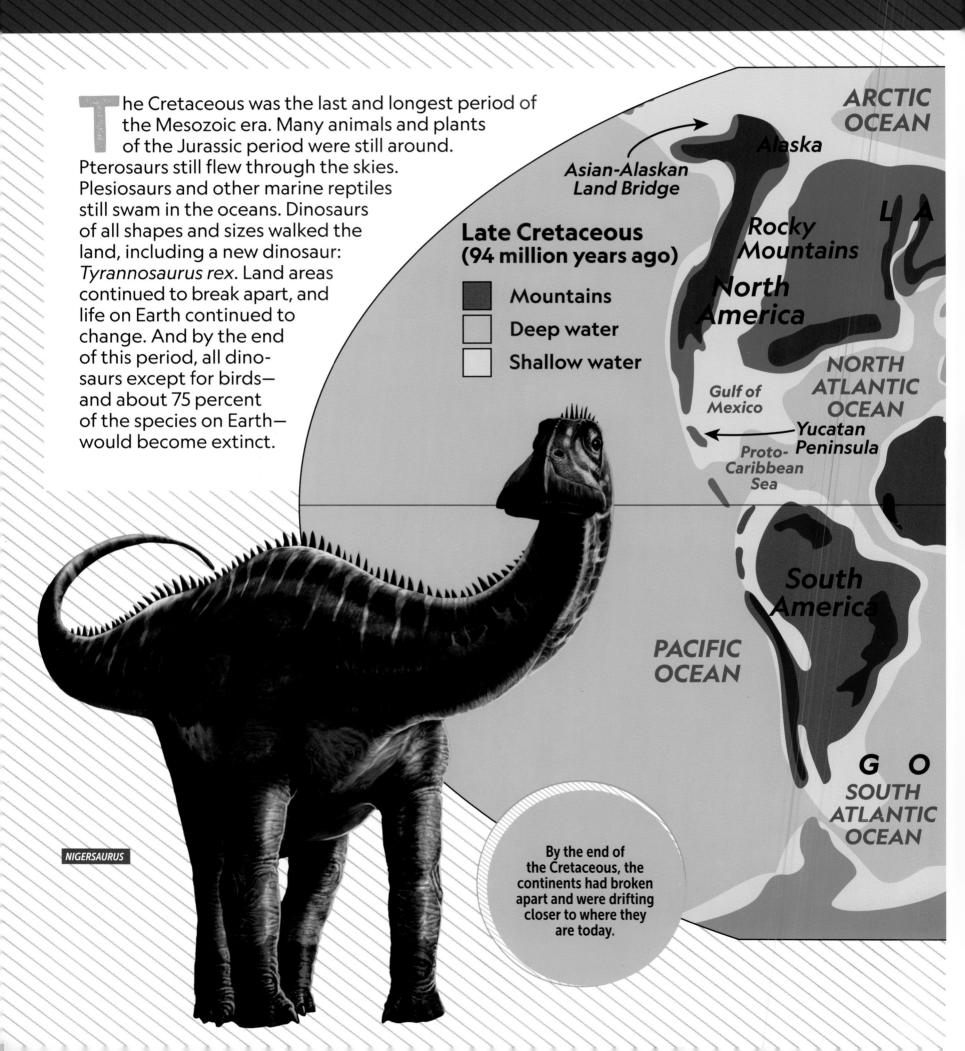

Late Cretaceous (94 million years ago)

- ■ Mountains
- □ Deep water
- □ Shallow water

ARCTIC OCEAN

Asian-Alaskan Land Bridge

Alaska

L A

Rocky Mountains

North America

NORTH ATLANTIC OCEAN

Gulf of Mexico

Yucatan Peninsula

Proto-Caribbean Sea

PACIFIC OCEAN

South America

G O

SOUTH ATLANTIC OCEAN

By the end of the Cretaceous, the continents had broken apart and were drifting closer to where they are today.

NIGERSAURUS

At the end of this period, an asteroid hit the Yucatan Peninsula in Mexico. Scientists believe this set off a chain of events that caused the mass extinction of the dinosaurs. Read more about this event on page 108.

India broke free from Gondwana during the Cretaceous period. About 50 million years ago, it drifted north and ran into Eurasia. This made the Himalaya mountains.

Australia and Antarctica were the last parts to break away from Gondwana. They moved away from each other 45 million years ago.

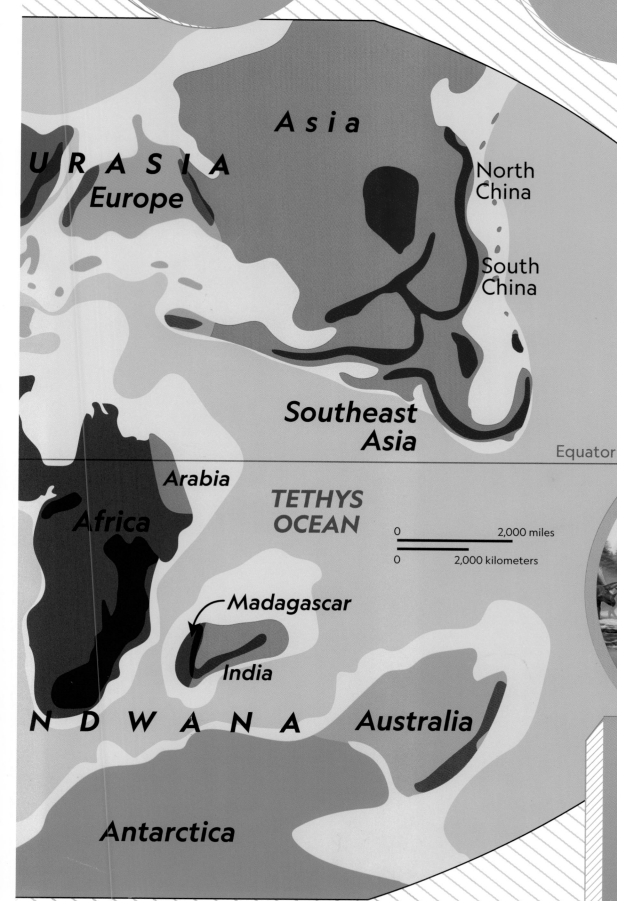

Asia

EURASIA
Europe

North China

South China

Southeast Asia

Equator

Arabia

TETHYS OCEAN

Africa

0 ———— 2,000 miles

0 ———— 2,000 kilometers

Madagascar

India

NDWANA

Australia

Antarctica

Could Dinosaurs Swim?

As continents spread apart and more bodies of water formed, dinosaurs may have gone swimming. Scientists found tracks preserved in ancient rivers that have since dried up. They look like dinosaur claws lightly touching the shallow river bottom.

CRETACEOUS HABITATS

As land areas kept shifting, the oceans, climate, and life on Earth continued to change. The first known flowering plants appeared during this period. There were now more kinds of habitats on Earth than ever before.

The Land

Plant life thrived on land. The ferns, gingkoes, and cycads of the past still thrived. And there were still evergreen trees and shrubs. But now the land was covered in plants that flowered, too. Colorful magnolias, sassafras, and ficus filled the forests.

While all of these plants and animals lived during this time, they would not likely have lived in the same place or even at the exact same time.

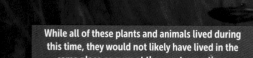

The Air

The Cretaceous was one of the warmest periods in Earth's history. But about halfway through the period, there was a six-million-year-long "cold snap" during which the weather became colder. Scientists think that as the continents shifted, the flow of the ocean might have changed, too. This might have affected the weather and made the planet colder. It is known as global cooling.

The water

Oceans were warm during the Cretaceous. Their temperatures may have reached as high as 95°F (35°C). Sea levels got higher and then lower over and over again. The high sea levels made the continent of Europe look like a bunch of small islands.

CRETACEOUS DINOSAURS

Lots of new kinds of dinosaurs appeared during the Cretaceous. Birds (avian dinosaurs) also became more common. Because the continents were now far apart from each other, dinosaurs in each place evolved in different ways. Some, like the long-necked sauropods, lived in both southern and northern lands. Others only lived in one area: The mighty *Tyrannosaurus rex* and horned *Triceratops* lived only in what is now North America.

IGUANODON
(ig-WHA-no-don)

MEANING: "Iguana tooth"

PERIOD: Early Cretaceous

LOCATION: Belgium; England

Iguanodon stood on four legs as it ate, but it could also walk on two legs. This dinosaur had a large spike on its thumb that scientists think it used to fight off predators and dig into fruits and seeds.

More Cretaceous Dinosaurs

Albertosaurus
(al-BERT-oh-SORE-us):
"Alberta lizard,"
Canada, Late Cretaceous

Beipiaosaurus
(BAY-pyow-SORE-us):
"Beipiao lizard,"
China, Early Cretaceous

Centrosaurus
(SEN-troh-SORE-us):
"Sharp pointed lizard,"
Canada, U.S.A.,
Late Cretaceous

CAUDIPTERYX
(CAW-dip-TEHR-iks)

MEANING: "Tail feather"

PERIOD: Early Cretaceous

LOCATION: China

This bird-like dinosaur had a tail with a fan of feathers at the end of it. It ate insects and plants with its beaked mouth. Its small, weak teeth were only at the top of its jaw.

ANKYLOSAURUS
(AN-kee-loh-SORE-us)

MEANING: "Stiff lizard"

PERIOD: LATE CRETACEOUS

LOCATION: Canada; U.S.A.

At 25 to 35 feet (7.6–10.6 m) long, *Ankylosaurus* was slow moving. But its hard, heavy tail could fight off a giant crocodile ... or a *T. rex!* And the strong armor on its back helped protect it from *T. rex*'s sharp teeth.

Edmontonia
(ed-mon-TONE-ee-ah):
"Of Edmonton,"
Canada, U.S.A.,
Late Cretaceous

Gallimimus
(gal-lee-MEEM-us):
"Chicken copy,"
Mongolia, Late Cretaceous

Saichania
(sie-CHAN-ee-a):
"Beautiful,"
Mongolia,
Late Cretaceous

CRETACEOUS LIFE

During the Cretaceous, other big changes came about. And they involved many animals besides dinosaurs. The first known flowering plants grew, and insects like butterflies appeared. They spread the pollen of these new flowering plants. Ants and wasps lived during the Cretaceous, too. Reptiles and amphibians—including frogs, turtles, crocodiles, snakes, and salamanders—spent time on the shores of the new continents. Pterosaurs continued to fly through the skies.

Sarcosuchus
(SAR-koh-SOO-kes)
Early Cretaceous

Sarcosuchus was one of the largest crocodiles ever known. It grew up to 40 feet (12 m) long—as long as a bus! And it weighed up to 15 tons (13.6 t). This huge reptile hunted dinosaurs on land and in water—including giant sauropods!

Snakes
Early Cretaceous through today

Many early snake-like creatures had tiny back legs they didn't use. These reptiles slithered on land and swam in the water. Their tiny needle-like teeth helped them catch prey, which they swallowed whole.

Aptenoperissus
(APT-ih-no-PEHR-iss-us)
Late Cretaceous

Scientists found this wingless wasp in an amber fossil in Myanmar. It had grasshopper-like legs, ant-like antennae, and a cockroach-like body. The unusual find didn't fit into any insect groups that scientists knew of. So scientists had to create a new one.

Quetzalcoatlus
(KET-sal-koh-AHT-lus)
Late Cretaceous

Quetzalcoatlus was about as tall as a giraffe. It had a wingspan up to 40 feet (12 m) wide. It was the largest flying reptile during the Cretaceous—and one of the largest flying animals to ever live on Earth!

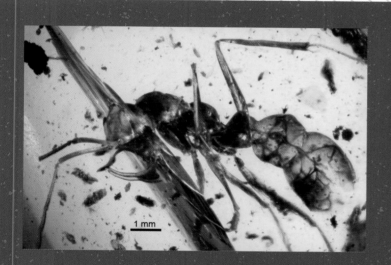

1 mm

Haidomyrmecinae
(HAI-doh-MIR-muh-seen)
Late Cretaceous

These ants were related to wasps. They weren't very big, measuring just 0.1 to 0.3 inch (0.3–0.8 cm) long. But they had fangs, which they used to bite other insects. Because of those fangs, scientists gave them the nickname "saber-toothed ants."

Mosasaurus (MOE-zah-SORE-us) Late Cretaceous

Mosasaurus was a fierce marine reptile. It could grow up to 49 feet (15 m) long. It swam through the ocean by moving its tail from side to side. It hunted fish, turtles, plesiosaurs, and even other smaller mosasaurs.

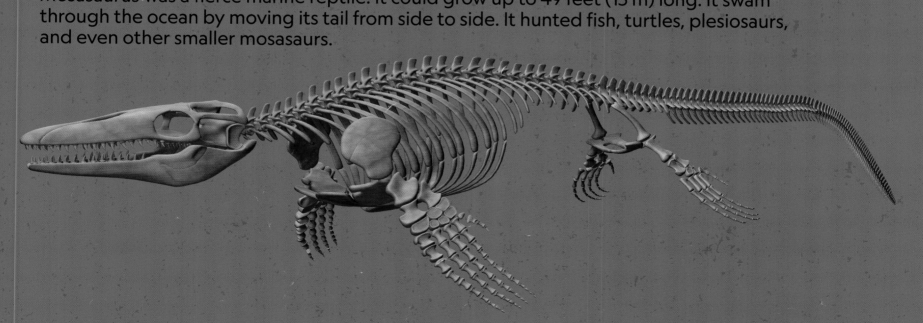

FINDING FOSSILS

NORTH AMERICA

North America has lots of great spots for hunting fossils. During the Jurassic and Cretaceous periods, much of today's American West was covered in water. It had coastlines, lakes, rivers, and shallow seas full of sand and mud, which could cover animals to make fossils. Millions of years later, these fossils came back to Earth's surface as rocks in parts of South Dakota and the Rocky Mountains. *Tyrannosaurus rex, Stegosaurus,* and *Triceratops* have been found only in North America.

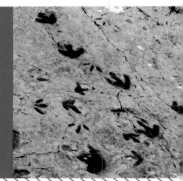

HELL CREEK
MONTANA, U.S.A.

Fossils of *Tyrannosaurus, Triceratops,* and many other Late Cretaceous dinosaurs have been found in these badlands. Badlands are dry places with soft rocks or soil and very few plants. Turn to page 50 for more info on this location.

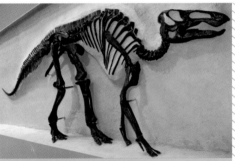

PRINCE CREEK FORMATION
ALASKA, U.S.A.

Thousands of bones from what experts believe may be young *Edmontosaurus* were found in this far-off part of northern Alaska. The location is one of the most northern places any dinosaur fossil has been found.

COMO BLUFF
WYOMING, U.S.A.

Stegosaurus, Allosaurus, and other dinosaur fossils were found here in quarries. Quarries are open mines from which rocks, sand, or minerals are taken from the earth.

MORRISON
COLORADO, U.S.A

One part of this area is nicknamed Dinosaur Ridge because so many fossils have been found here, including the first *Stegosaurus* discovery.

RED DEER RIVER
ALBERTA, CANADA

The fossils of more than 50 dinosaur species, such as *Albertosaurus* and *Corythosaurus,* have been found in Dinosaur Provincial Park. Learn more about this public park on page 52.

DINOSAUR NATIONAL MONUMENT
Utah and Colorado, U.S.A.

Fossils of large plant-eaters like *Apatosaurus* and meat-eaters like *Allosaurus* have been found here. Visitors can see fossils "in-situ," which means the fossils are still in the rocks in the ground.

GHOST RANCH
NEW MEXICO, U.S.A.

A "graveyard" of several hundred *Coelophysis* skeletons was found here in 1947. Turn to page 54 to learn more about this important site.

More Dinosaurs of North America

Chirostenotes
(kie-ROH-sten-OH-teez):
"Narrow-handed,"
Canada, Late Cretaceous

Dryosaurus
(dry-oh-SORE-us):
"Oak lizard,"
U.S.A., Late Jurassic

Leptoceratops
(lep-toh-SEHR-uh-tops):
"Slim horned face,"
Canada, U.S.A.,
Late Cretaceous

ARCTIC OCEAN

Greenland
(Kalaallit Nunaat)
(Denmark)

Prince Creek
Formation

Alaska
(U.S.)

PALUXY RIVER
TEXAS, U.S.A.

A trackway found here is from the Early Cretaceous period. It is made of two sets of fossilized footprints: one from a large plant-eater and one from a large meat-eater.

COAHUILA
MEXICO

Duck-billed dinosaurs from the Cretaceous have been found in this area, including a young *Velafrons* with nostrils in unusual spots. Learn more on page 56.

CANADA

PACIFIC
OCEAN

Red Deer
River Valley
Alberta

Hell Creek
Formation
Montana

Como Bluff
Wyoming

UNITED
STATES

Dinosaur
National Monument
Utah and Colorado

Morrison
Colorado

ATLANTIC
OCEAN

Ghost Ranch
New Mexico

Paluxy River
Texas

THE
BAHAMAS

West Indies

Coahuila

Gulf of
Mexico

CUBA

DOMINICAN
REPUBLIC

ANTIGUA &
BARBUDA

Map Key

● Point of interest

▮ Area of interest

The color of each point or area of interest matches its specific caption color on the page.

0   600 miles

0   600 kilometers

MEXICO

HAITI

ST. KITTS
& NEVIS
ST. LUCIA

DOMINICA

BARBADOS

JAMAICA

Caribbean Sea

GRENADA

ST. VINCENT &
THE GRENADINES

TRINIDAD &
TOBAGO

BELIZE
HONDURAS

GUATEMALA

NICARAGUA

EL SALVADOR

COSTA RICA

PANAMA

Parasaurolophus
(PA-ra-sore-OL-off-us):
"Like *Saurolophus*,"
Canada, U.S.A.,
Late Cretaceous

Troodon
(TROH-oh-don):
"Damaging tooth,"
U.S.A., Late Cretaceous

Zuniceratops
(ZOO-nee-SEHR-uh-tops):
"Zuni-horned face,"
U.S.A., Late Cretaceous

SPOTLIGHT ON:
HELL CREEK, MONTANA, U.S.A.

FOSSIL FINDS: *TRICERATOPS, TYRANNOSAURUS*
WHEN: CRETACEOUS

← **Montana**

UNITED STATES

During the Late Cretaceous period, Hell Creek wasn't the dry, rocky badlands it is today. It was a large, wet, and forested area where rivers drained into the sea. It was full of palm trees, redwoods, and flowering plants. Over time, the area changed. Sediment (tiny pieces of plants, minerals, and animals) hardened into rock hundreds of feet thick. The sediment from different time periods looks different, making the colorful stripes in gray, pink, green, and blue we see today.

HELL CREEK

TRICERATOPS (try-SEHR-uh-tops)

MEANING: "Three horned face"

PERIOD: Late Cretaceous

Growing up to 30 feet (8 m) long, *Triceratops* was the last and largest known horned dinosaur. It had a three-foot (1-m)-long frill and three horns. Scientists think it may have used its horns to scare off predators like the tyrannosaurs, although they may have only been for show. The frill may have protected its neck or may have attracted mates. This slow-moving herbivore had 800 tiny teeth. It used them to eat plants.

TRICERATOPS FOSSIL FOUND IN HELL CREEK, MONTANA

Map Key

★ State capital
○ Point of interest
□ Area of interest

0 — 50 miles
0 — 50 kilometers

Hell Creek Formation

M o n t a n a

Helena ★

U N I T E D   S T A T E S

Museum of the Rockies ○

TYRANNOSAURUS
(tie-RAN-oh-SORE-us)

MEANING: "Tyrant lizard"

PERIOD: Late Cretaceous

Hell Creek became famous to paleontologists in 1902. That's when fossil collector Barnum Brown found the first fossil of a *Tyrannosaurus*. This mighty dinosaur could grow to 40 feet (12 m) long. It wasn't the biggest or the fastest dinosaur. It could only run up to 12 miles an hour (19 km/h). But it was strong. Its jaws could smash the bones of almost any animal.

DINO DISCOVERER:
Jack Horner

Jack Horner is a famous American paleontologist. Horner and his team found the first evidence of a big dinosaur nesting ground. They have spent more than 40 summers at Hell Creek. They dodged rattlesnakes, 100°F (37°C) heat, and strong winds as they hunted for fossils. Many of the fossils Horner and his team found are kept at the Museum of the Rockies in nearby Bozeman, Montana.

SPOTLIGHT ON:
DINOSAUR PROVINCIAL PARK
ALBERTA, CANADA

FOSSIL FINDS: *CHASMOSAURUS, CORYTHOSAURUS*
WHEN: CRETACEOUS

CANADA

← Alberta

Dinosaur Provincial Park is in the Red Deer River Valley of Alberta, Canada. During the Cretaceous, this land was hot and humid. It was filled with forests and rivers. Now, these are dry badlands with steep hills of rock. These hills have been worn away over time by wind and water. Since 1889, fossils of more than 400 animals have been discovered here. This includes more than 50 species of dinosaurs. There are so many fossils that scientists think this area may have fossils from more kinds of Cretaceous land animals than anywhere else.

DINOSAUR PROVINCIAL PARK

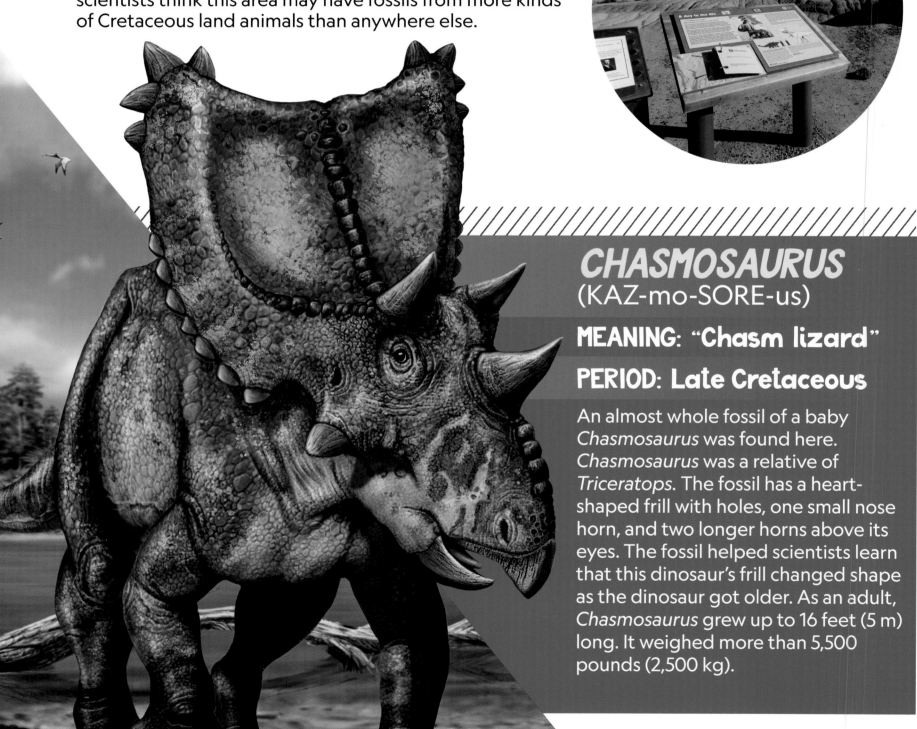

CHASMOSAURUS
(KAZ-mo-SORE-us)

MEANING: "Chasm lizard"

PERIOD: Late Cretaceous

An almost whole fossil of a baby *Chasmosaurus* was found here. *Chasmosaurus* was a relative of *Triceratops*. The fossil has a heart-shaped frill with holes, one small nose horn, and two longer horns above its eyes. The fossil helped scientists learn that this dinosaur's frill changed shape as the dinosaur got older. As an adult, *Chasmosaurus* grew up to 16 feet (5 m) long. It weighed more than 5,500 pounds (2,500 kg).

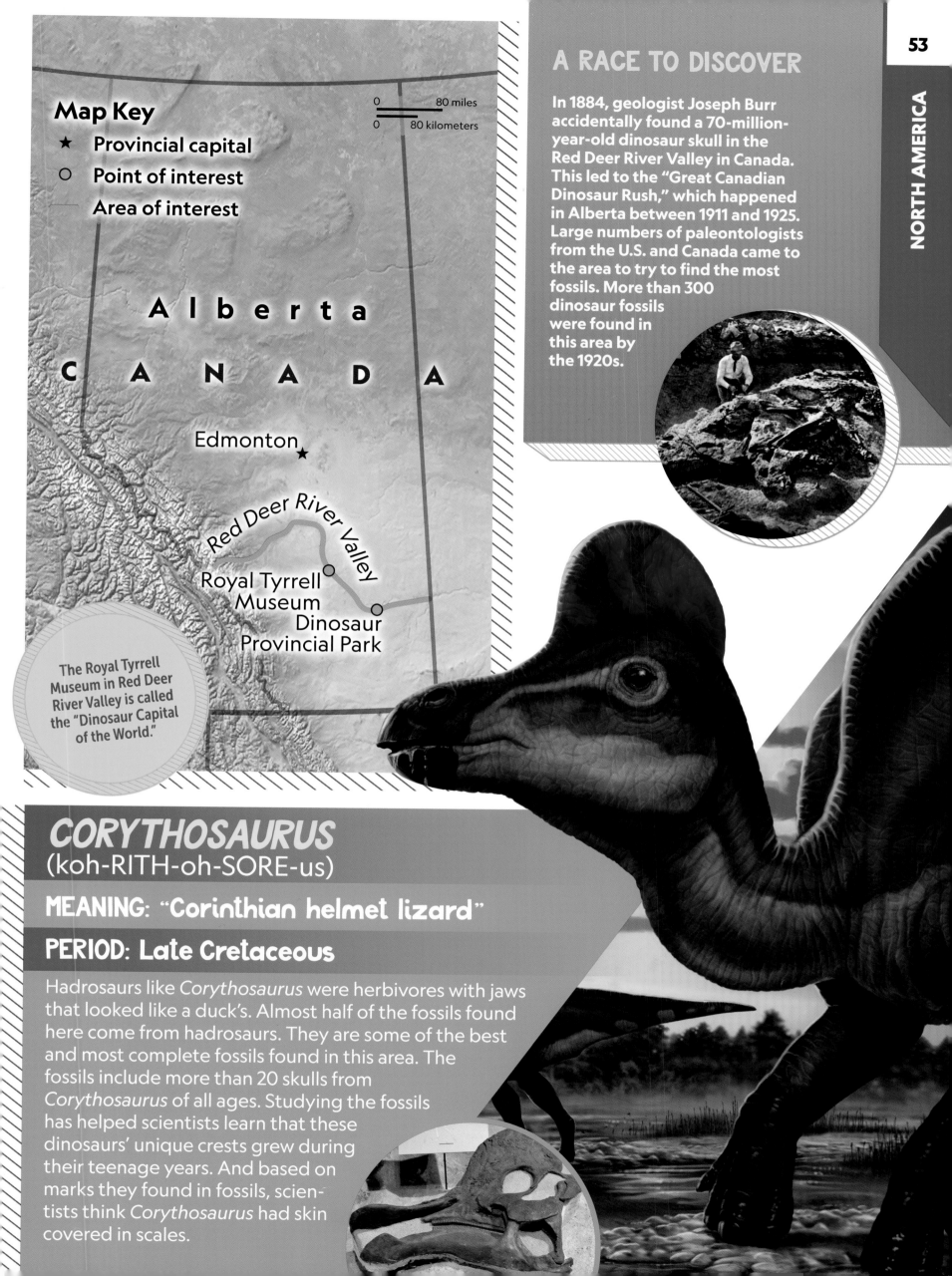

Map Key
★ Provincial capital
○ Point of interest
— Area of interest

0 ___ 80 miles
0 ___ 80 kilometers

A l b e r t a

C A N A D A

Edmonton ★

Red Deer River Valley

Royal Tyrrell Museum

Dinosaur Provincial Park

The Royal Tyrrell Museum in Red Deer River Valley is called the "Dinosaur Capital of the World."

A RACE TO DISCOVER

In 1884, geologist Joseph Burr accidentally found a 70-million-year-old dinosaur skull in the Red Deer River Valley in Canada. This led to the "Great Canadian Dinosaur Rush," which happened in Alberta between 1911 and 1925. Large numbers of paleontologists from the U.S. and Canada came to the area to try to find the most fossils. More than 300 dinosaur fossils were found in this area by the 1920s.

CORYTHOSAURUS
(koh-RITH-oh-SORE-us)

MEANING: "Corinthian helmet lizard"

PERIOD: Late Cretaceous

Hadrosaurs like *Corythosaurus* were herbivores with jaws that looked like a duck's. Almost half of the fossils found here come from hadrosaurs. They are some of the best and most complete fossils found in this area. The fossils include more than 20 skulls from *Corythosaurus* of all ages. Studying the fossils has helped scientists learn that these dinosaurs' unique crests grew during their teenage years. And based on marks they found in fossils, scientists think *Corythosaurus* had skin covered in scales.

SPOTLIGHT ON:
GHOST RANCH, NEW MEXICO, U.S.A.

FOSSIL FINDS: *COELOPHYSIS, TAWA*
WHEN: TRIASSIC AND JURASSIC

UNITED STATES
← New Mexico

At Ghost Ranch, the red cliffs are filled with fossils of early dinosaurs. There are fossils of animals that came before dinosaurs, too. The mix of fossils at this site helped scientists prove that dinosaurs weren't always the most common land animal on Earth. In fact, the fossils helped scientists learn that it took tens of millions of years for dinosaurs to evolve into the creatures that ruled the Jurassic and Cretaceous periods.

GHOST RANCH

In 1998, a *Coelophysis* skull was sent to space on the shuttle *Endeavor!*

COELOPHYSIS (SEE-low-FY-sis)

MEANING: "Hollow form"

PERIOD: LateTriassic to Early Jurassic

Coelophysis walked on two legs. It had curved claws and small, sharp teeth. It also had limbs with hollow bones. At less than 6.5 feet (2 m) long and about 66 pounds (30 kg), it was a small carnivore. But it was fast, moving up to 25 to 30 miles an hour (40–48 km/h). That speed helped this hunter catch food such as insects and small reptiles and amphibians.

ART ALL AROUND

Artist Georgia O'Keeffe lived at Ghost Ranch for many years. A lot of her paintings are landscapes, or paintings of the land. Scientists named a Late Triassic fossil, *Effigia okeeffeae,* after her. Scientists originally thought the animal was a two-legged dinosaur. But after looking at it more, they learned it was actually related to today's alligators and crocodiles.

0   60 miles
0   60 kilometers

Ghost Ranch

Santa Fe

New Mexico

U N I T E D   S T A T E S

Map Key

★   State capital

○   Point of interest

TAWA (ta-wa)

MEANING:
"Big hollow"

PERIOD: LateTriassic

Rare fossils of a dinosaur that was
213 to 215 million years old were found
in New Mexico in 2004. *Tawa* had a
body the size of a large dog and a
long neck and tail. Its sharp, curved
teeth showed that it was one of the
very first meat-eating dinosaurs
to walk the planet.

Coelophysis
is the official
state dinosaur
of New Mexico.

SPOTLIGHT ON:
COAHUILA, MEXICO

FOSSIL FINDS: *VELAFRONS, COAHUILACERATOPS*
WHEN: CRETACEOUS

NORTH AMERICA

MEXICO

Today, this part of northern Mexico is a dry desert. But from the Late Jurassic to the Late Cretaceous, it was a busy marshland. During that time, the area was humid and full of plants. The sea was full of life, from turtles to crocodiles to dinosaurs to clams. Today, fossils from both the land and the sea have been found here. This includes those of at least 14 species of dinosaurs.

COAHUILA

VELAFRONS
(VEHL-uh-fronz)

MEANING:
"Sailed forehead"

PERIOD:
Late Cretaceous

Like other hadrosaurs, *Velafrons* had a rounded crest on its skull. But its nose bone rested on top of its skull instead of in front of its eyes. The fossil found at Coahuila was from a young *Velafrons* that would have been 25 feet (8 m) long. Adults may have grown to be 35 feet (11 m) long. It took several years to carefully take this fossil from the ground after it was found in 1992.

A TALL TAIL!

Many hadrosaur fossils have been found in this area. But when a 16-foot (5-m)-long hadrosaur tail was found in 2012, it was extra exciting. This was the first dinosaur tail found in Mexico. The tail was made of 50 vertebrae, which are connected bones in the spine. Scientists also found a hip bone from the same dinosaur. They hope the fossil will help them learn how hadrosaur tails moved.

PACIFIC
OCEAN

Coahuila

Gulf of
Mexico

Mexico

Mexico City ✪

Caribbean
Sea

Map Key

✪ Capital

◻ Area of interest

0 ——— 200 miles
0 ——— 200 kilometers

COAHUILACERATOPS
(koh-WHEE-lah-SEHR-uh-tops)

MEANING: "Horn face from Coahuila"

PERIOD: Late Cretaceous

Coahuilaceratops was a herbivore about the size of a rhino at 22 feet (7 m) long and four to five tons (3.6–4.5 t). Two extra-large horns grew from its six-foot (2-m)-long skull—one above each eye. The horns may have been three to four feet (0.9–1.2 m) long. That means this dinosaur had one of the largest eye-horns of all the ceratopsians.

COAHUILACERATOPS SKULL

SOUTH AMERICA

S outh America was part of the southern supercontinent called Gondwana. Gondwana began to break apart about 200 million years ago. About 150 million years ago, South America moved away from Africa. It was soon far off by itself. The dinosaurs here evolved into species that were different from dinosaurs on other continents. Scientists think that may be why South American sauropods were so big. They are some of Earth's largest dinosaurs.

PLAZA HUINCUL
ARGENTINA

In 1987, a local man found a bone. He had no idea that it was from the *Argentinosaurus,* the largest dinosaur found at that time. The dinosaur may have been 98.4 feet (30 m) long and 32.8 feet (10 m) tall.

SÃO PAULO STATE
BRAZIL

The spine of an 82-foot (25-m)-long *Austroposeidon* from the Cretaceous was found here. It was the one of the largest and most complete titanosaurs ever found in Brazil.

VENEZUELAN ANDES
VENEZUELA

The first dinosaur fossil ever found in Venezuela was a group of four *Laquintasaura,* a new species that researchers announced in 2014. Learn more on page 66.

AYSÉN REGION
CHILE

A small two-legged herbivore, the *Chilesaurus diegosuarezi,* was found here in 2004 by a seven-year-old boy. It is named after the place it was found and the boy who discovered it. See page 61 to learn more.

BOYACÁ
COLOMBIA

A plesiosaur fossil from the Cretaceous was found in 2013 in this area, which was underwater 130 million years ago. The fossil was 33 feet (10 m) long. It had a long neck, a short tail, and a flat body.

More Dinosaurs of South America

Antarctosaurus
(ant-ARK-toe-SORE-us):
"Antarctic lizard,"
Argentina, Chile, Uruguay,
Late Cretaceous

Chubutisaurus
(choo-boot-i-SORE-us):
"Chubut [Province] lizard,"
Argentina,
Early Cretaceous

Giganotosaurus
(gig-an-OH-toe-SORE-us):
"Giant southern lizard,"
Argentina, Late Cretaceous

Learn more on page 62.

Caribbean Sea

Venezuelan Andes

VENEZUELA

Boyacá

COLOMBIA

French Guiana (France)

GUYANA

SURINAME

ECUADOR

Galápagos Islands (Ecuador)

PERU

BRAZIL

RIO GRANDE DO SUL
BRAZIL

Three long-necked, plant-eating *Macrocollum* dinosaur fossils were found here. They were very well preserved. They are among the oldest long-necked dinosaurs that we know of.

BOLIVIA

São Paulo

PARAGUAY

Rio Grande do Sul

CHILE

ATLANTIC OCEAN

URUGUAY

PACIFIC OCEAN

ARGENTINA

○ Plaza Huincul

Map Key

● Point of interest

▮ Area of interest

The color of each point or area of interest matches its specific caption color on the page.

0 ——— 500 miles

0 ——— 500 kilometers

P a t a g o n i a

Aysén

Falkland Islands (*Islas Malvinas*) (U.K.)

PATAGONIA
ARGENTINA

Scientists think the world's largest dinosaur (and maybe land animal ever) was a titanosaur named *Patagotitan*. Learn more on page 62.

Arctic Ocean

North America

Atlantic Ocean

Europe

Asia

Pacific Ocean

Africa

South America

Indian Ocean

Pacific Ocean

Australia & Oceania

Southern Ocean

Antarctica

Mussaurus
(moos-SORE-us):
"Mouse lizard,"
Argentina,
Late Triassic

Irritator
(IRR-it-ate-or):
"Irritator," Brazil,
Early Cretaceous

Saltasaurus
(SALT-ah-SORE-us):
"Salta lizard," Argentina,
Late Cretaceous

SPOTLIGHT ON:
CHILE

FOSSIL FINDS: *ATACAMATITAN, CHILESAURUS*
WHEN: JURASSIC AND CRETACEOUS

SOUTH AMERICA

CHILE →

The dinosaur fossils found in Chile are mostly from titanosaurs. Most are fossils from about 72 to 66 million years ago (just before the dinosaur-destroying meteor struck). There are many fossils along the border that Chile shares with Argentina. There are fossils of Cretaceous flowers, leaves, and marine reptiles like plesiosaurs.

During the Cretaceous, sea levels dropped because the climate changed. This lower water uncovered a land bridge between South America and Antarctica. This bridge meant that dinosaurs and other animals could travel between these places.

MOON VALLEY, CHILE

ATACAMATITAN
(AT-ah-COM-uh-TIE-tin)

MEANING: "Giant from the Atacama Desert"

PERIOD: Late Cretaceous

This new species of titanosaur was found in the Atacama Desert of northern Chile in 2001, when paleontologists saw a leg bone sticking out of the red sandstone. Even though very few bones were found, it is still one of the most complete titanosaur fossils found in Chile. From the size of the leg bone, scientists think this titanosaur may have weighed 5.6 tons (5 t).

Map Key

⊛ Capital

☐ Area of interest

Atacama Desert

s
e
n
d
A

Chile

⊛ Santiago

PACIFIC OCEAN

Aysén

ATLANTIC OCEAN

0 300 miles
0 300 kilometers

DISCOVERED BY A KID!

In 2004, seven-year-old Diego Suarez joined his parents on a trip to the southern Aysén Region of Chile. While his parents were studying rocks in the Andes mountains, Diego found a fossil! Soon his geologist parents and other scientists began looking at the fossil site. The group found more than 12 turkey-size fossils. Five of the skeletons were complete! They named this dinosaur *Chilesaurus diegosuarezi* after Chile, the place it was found, and Diego Suarez, who first found it.

Chilesaurus was the first complete dinosaur from the Jurassic period found in Chile. Scientists are still trying to figure out if it is an ornithischian or a theropod.

CHILESAURUS (CHEE-lay-SORE-us)

MEANING: "Chile lizard"

PERIOD: Late Jurassic

Found in southern Chile, *Chilesaurus* has been nicknamed a "Frankenstein dinosaur" or "platypus dinosaur." It had a lot of body parts that looked different from each other (just like Frankenstein's monster or a platypus!). This turkey-size, plant-eating dinosaur had short arms and a long tail. It had a long neck, and it walked on two legs. Although it looked strange to the scientists who studied it, it was the most common animal around when it was alive.

SPOTLIGHT ON:
PATAGONIA, ARGENTINA

FOSSIL FINDS: *PATAGOTITAN, ARGENTINOSAURUS*
WHEN: CRETACEOUS

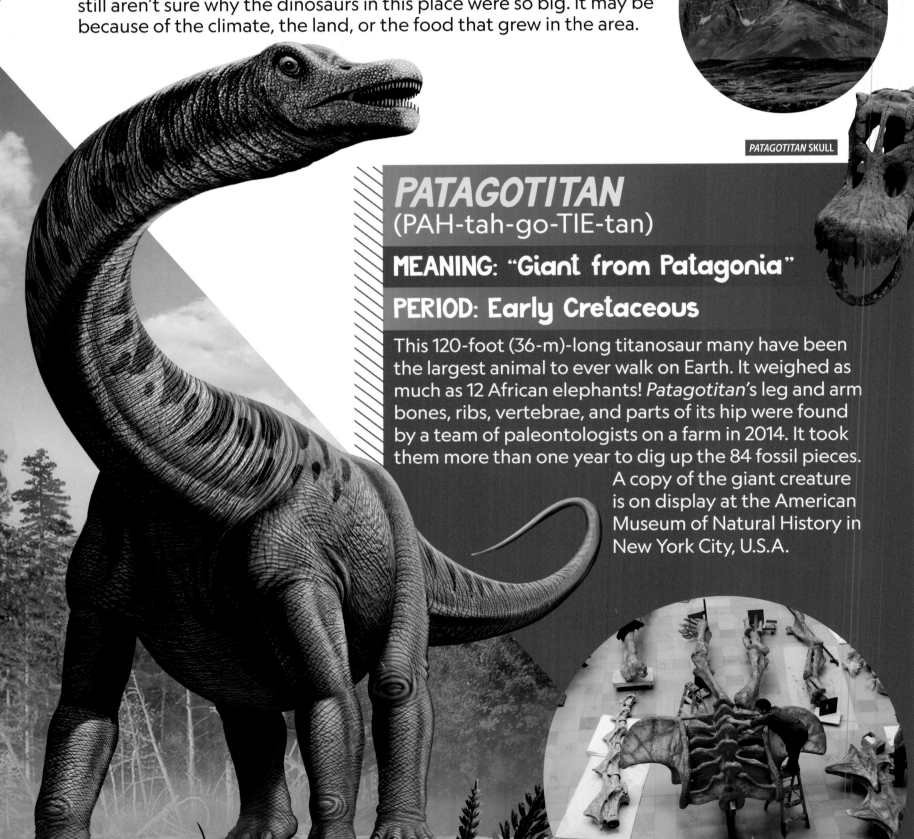

SOUTH AMERICA

CHILE →

← ARGENTINA

Patagonia

South America has some of the biggest dinosaur fossils of all time. They are mostly found in one area: Patagonia. This is a place in Chile and Argentina where the Andes run between the two countries. Like other places around the world where fossils are found, the Argentinian side of Patagonia is a desert badlands. The dirt and rocks have worn away, which makes it easier to spot fossils. Scientists still aren't sure why the dinosaurs in this place were so big. It may be because of the climate, the land, or the food that grew in the area.

PATAGONIA

PATAGOTITAN SKULL

PATAGOTITAN
(PAH-tah-go-TIE-tan)

MEANING: "Giant from Patagonia"

PERIOD: Early Cretaceous

This 120-foot (36-m)-long titanosaur many have been the largest animal to ever walk on Earth. It weighed as much as 12 African elephants! *Patagotitan*'s leg and arm bones, ribs, vertebrae, and parts of its hip were found by a team of paleontologists on a farm in 2014. It took them more than one year to dig up the 84 fossil pieces. A copy of the giant creature is on display at the American Museum of Natural History in New York City, U.S.A.

THE GIANT TITANOSAURS

Titanosaurs, a group of sauropods including *Dreadnoughtus*, *Argentinosaurus*, and *Patagotitan*, were huge. They had big bodies and small heads. Their very long necks helped them reach plants and leaves up high. With tiny teeth, they may not have been able to chew, so they may have swallowed mouthfuls of plants whole. Titanosaurs walked on four legs, but they were so heavy that they had to be careful with each step. Their bones could break if they moved too fast.

Map Key
- ⊛ Capital
- ▢ Area of interest

Andes

Argentina

Santiago
Chile

Buenos Aires ⊛

PACIFIC OCEAN

Andes

Patagonia

ATLANTIC OCEAN

0   300 miles
0   300 kilometers

ARGENTINOSAURUS
(AR-gen-TEEN-oh-SORE-us)

MEANING: "Argentina lizard"

PERIOD: Late Cretaceous

Scientists think this huge 121-foot (37-m)-long herbivore might have needed to eat about 100,000 calories per day—that's 50 whole chocolate cakes! And it may have had weak jaws and thin teeth that could help it rip the leaves off trees. But scientists aren't sure, because an *Argentinosaurus* skull has never been found.

SPOTLIGHT ON:
RIO GRANDE DO SUL, BRAZIL

FOSSIL FINDS: *MACROCOLLUM, BAGUALOSAURUS*
WHEN: TRIASSIC

BRAZIL
SOUTH AMERICA

Important fossils from at least seven Triassic-period dinosaur species have been found in this southern part of Brazil. Triassic fossils are rare because they are so old. Skeletons this old are rarely found whole or unbroken. But South America—in Brazil and Argentina—is where most of these early dinosaurs have been found. Some are from 230 million years ago!

RIO GRANDE DO SUL

MACROCOLLUM (MACK-row-COLL-um)

MEANING: "Long neck"

PERIOD: Late Triassic

Macrocollum was a small two-legged dinosaur that could move fast. It was 11 feet (3 m) long. That may seem extra small when you know that these early dinosaurs were related to huge, long-necked, four-legged sauropods. Scientists hope *Macrocollum* will help them learn how sauropods grew so big. *Macrocollum* is the oldest known long-necked sauropodomorph.

MACROCOLLUM ITAQUII FOSSIL

0 — 500 miles
0 — 500 kilometers

B r a z i l

PACIFIC OCEAN

⍟Brasília

ATLANTIC OCEAN

Map Key
⊛ Capital
☐ Area of interest

Rio Grande do Sul

BAGUALOSAURUS
(bag-WALL-oh-SORE-us)

MEANING: "Strongly built lizard"

PERIOD: Late Triassic

BAGUALOSAURUS AGUDOENSIS FOSSIL

At eight feet (2.5 m) long, the *Bagualosaurus* was large for the time. Other early sauropodomorphs were only about five feet (1.5 m) long. But that's not the only way it was different. Scientists think *Bagualosaurus* ate mostly plants. Other Late Triassic dinosaurs were omnivores. Like *Macrocollum,* this newly discovered dinosaur has helped scientists find out how early dinosaurs evolved into larger plant-eating sauropods like the *Brachiosaurus.*

WHAT BONES CAN TELL US

Three fossils are better than one! And three fossils found in the same place means something to paleontologists. In 2012, paleontologists found three *Macrocollum itaquii* fossils together in southern Brazil. This means these dinosaurs may have died at the same time near each other. That makes paleontologists think they may have lived together. This may mean that some dinosaurs liked to be around each other instead of being alone.

SPOTLIGHT ON:
LA QUINTA FORMATION, VENEZUELA

FOSSIL FINDS: *TACHIRAPTOR, LAQUINTASAURA*
WHEN: JURASSIC

← VENEZUELA

SOUTH AMERICA

Fossils help scientists learn about extinct animals. They also provide information about the animals' habitats—the land, weather, and plants around them. That's why *Laquintasaura venezuelae* was such an important find. There was a huge extinction at the end of the Triassic period. But the *Laquintasaura* fossils showed that dinosaurs survived and grew strong again. Based on the age of the rocks the fossils were found in, dinosaurs were doing well again just 500,000 years after that extinction. (That's fast in dinosaur time!)

NEAR LA QUINTA FORMATION

TACHIRAPTOR
(TAW-chee-RAP-tor)

MEANING: "Thief of Táchira"

PERIOD: Early Jurassic

Only a leg bone and hip bone of this dinosaur were found in 2013. But the find was still exciting. Not very many dinosaurs had been found in this northern part of South America. Even with just part of a skeleton, paleontologists learned that this small theropod was about the size of a wolf, at five feet (1.5 m) long. As a two-legged meat-eater, it may have eaten any small creature it met—including *Laquintasaura*.

In the novel *The Lost World* by Arthur Conan Doyle, dinosaurs attack a group of explorers on a South American mountain. This scene might be inspired by Venezuela's Mount Roraima, but no dinosaur fossils have been found there yet.

Map Key
⊛ Capital
○ Point of interest

Caribbean Sea

0 — 100 miles
0 — 100 kilometers

Caracas ⊛

ATLANTIC OCEAN

V e n e z u e l a

○ La Quinta Formation

Mount Roraima ○

Equator —————————————————————— 0°

LAQUINTASAURA
(lah-KWEEN-tuh-SORE-uh)

MEANING: "Lizard of La Quinta"

PERIOD: Early Jurassic

Laquintasaura, the first dinosaur found in Venezuela, was the size of a small dog. It was about three feet (1 m) long and walked on two legs. Its teeth were long, narrow, and shaped like triangles. The teeth had curved tips and jagged edges, like knives. Scientists think *Laquintasaura* ate ferns and small prey, such as insects.

LIFE ON THE EQUATOR

By studying the rocks near the Equator in South America, scientists learned what the area was like 201 million years ago. The rock layers showed scientists that the height of the water in this place changed over time. Sometimes the region was a hot desert. Other times it was swampy. Scientists at first thought this meant dinosaurs would not have been able to survive here. But somehow *Laquintasaura* and *Tachiraptor* did! More fossils will need to be found before scientists can figure out how.

EUROPE

During the Jurassic period, the supercontinent Pangaea broke apart into Laurasia and Gondwana. As these two smaller supercontinents moved farther apart, the ocean rose between them, forming the Tethys Sea. During the Late Cretaceous, today's Europe was a group of islands in the Tethys Sea called the Tethyan Archipelago.

ISLE OF SKYE
SCOTLAND

It's called "Dinosaur Island" for a reason— there are tons of dinosaur footprints along the coast that can be seen during low tide.

ISLE OF WIGHT
ENGLAND

Lots of Early Cretaceous dinosaurs were found here, including *Hypsilophodon*, *Neovenator*, *Iguanodon*, and many other species.

SURREY
ENGLAND

In 1983, a crocodile-like fossil called *Baryonyx* was found. It had a giant claw and spent time catching fish in the water and looking for food on shore.

JURASSIC COAST
UNITED KINGDOM

The English Channel coastline is a great place to find marine fossils from all periods in the Mesozoic era. Learn more about it on page 70.

AIX-EN-PROVENCE
FRANCE

Thousands of dinosaur eggs have been found here. So have *Rhabdodon* fossils, a common dinosaur nicknamed the "Cretaceous cow." Learn more on page 76.

BERNISSART
BELGIUM

About 30 well-preserved *Iguanodon* fossils were accidentally found here in 1878 in a coal mine. They weren't the first *Iguanodon* ever found, but lots of the fossils in this find were almost complete.

More Dinosaurs of Europe

Dacentrurus
(DAH-sen-TROO-russ): "Pointed tail," United Kingdom, Late Jurassic

Juravenator
(ju-RAH-ve-NAY-tor): "Hunter from Jura," Germany, Late Jurassic

Polacanthus
(pol-a-KAN-thus): "Many spines," United Kingdom, Early Cretaceous

BAKONYJÁKÓ
HUNGARY

Hungarosaurus, Ajkaceratops, and other Cretaceous fossils were found in the Bakony mountains of Hungary. Turn to page 72 to learn more about this fossil site.

BAVARIA
GERMANY

Plateosaurus, Archaeopteryx, and lots of Late Jurassic plants, fish, and other animals have been found in Bavaria, Germany. Learn more on page 74.

TRANSYLVANIA
ROMANIA

Balaur bondoc ("stocky dragon") is a *Velociraptor* relative that lived in the Late Cretaceous. This meat-eater was about the size of a poodle, with two large sickle-shaped claws on each foot. It was found in 2009.

ICELAND

Barents Sea

SWEDEN
NORWAY
FINLAND

RUSSIA

Isle of Skye **Scotland**
North Sea

IRELAND (ÉIRE)
UNITED KINGDOM
ESTONIA

Isle of Wight **England**
DENMARK
LATVIA
LITHUANIA
RUSSIA

Jurassic Coast **England** — **Surrey England**
NETH.
BELARUS

ATLANTIC OCEAN
English Channel
BELGIUM
GERMANY
POLAND

Bernissart
LUXEMBOURG
Bavaria
CZECHIA (CZECH REP.)
UKRAINE

KAZAKHSTAN

LIECHTENSTEIN
AUSTRIA
SLOVAKIA

Bay of Biscay
FRANCE
SWITZ.
Bakonyjákó
HUNGARY
MOLDOVA
Caspian Sea

SLOVENIA
Transylvania
ROMANIA

Aix-en-Provence
ITALY
MONACO
CROATIA
SLOVENIA
GEORGIA

PORTUGAL
ANDORRA
SAN MARINO
BOSNIA & HERZEGOVINA
SERBIA
Black Sea
AZERBAIJAN

SPAIN
VATICAN CITY
MONTENEGRO
KOSOVO
BULGARIA

ALBANIA
NORTH MACEDONIA
TURKEY

MALTA
GREECE
CYPRUS

Mediterranean Sea

```
0        400 miles
0        400 kilometers
```

Map Key

♦ Small country

● Point of interest

▇ Area of interest

The color of each point or area of interest matches its specific caption color on the page.

Europasaurus
(yoo-ROH-pah-SORE-us):
"Europe lizard,"
Germany, Late Jurassic

Pelecanimimus
(pel-e-kan-i-MIM-us):
"Pelican copy,"
Spain, Early Cretaceous

Struthiosaurus
(STROO-thee-oh-SORE-us):
"Ostrich lizard,"
Austria, France, Romania, and Spain, Late Cretaceous

SPOTLIGHT ON:
JURASSIC COAST, U.K.

FOSSIL FINDS: *SCELIDOSAURUS*, AMMONITES
WHEN: TRIASSIC, JURASSIC, AND CRETACEOUS

UNITED KINGDOM

EUROPE

Almost 200 million years of history can be found in southwestern England at the Jurassic Coast. Fossils of fish, insects, reptiles, and plants from throughout the Mesozoic era are here. They can be found in layers of rock from all three periods. The Jurassic Coast stretches about 100 miles (160 km) across towns and beaches. Visitors can hunt for fossils and see the cliffs. This area has lots of marine fossils because it was under the sea during parts of the Jurassic and Cretaceous periods.

JURASSIC COAST

Although dinosaur fossils are rare in this spot, fossils of dinosaur footprints from the Cretaceous period have been found.

SCELIDOSAURUS
(skel-EYE-doh-SORE-us)

MEANING: "Limb lizard"

PERIOD: Early Jurassic

Dinosaur fossils on the Jurassic Coast are rare, as it was mostly underwater during the Mesozoic era. But some dinosaur fossils have been found. Two almost whole skeletons of a dinosaur named *Scelidosaurus* were found in the 1850s. Bumpy scales ran down the neck, back, and tail of this 13-foot (4-m)-long plant-eater. The fossils were studied later by Richard Owen, the man who first came up with the word "dinosaur."

SCELIDOSAURUS HAND FOSSIL

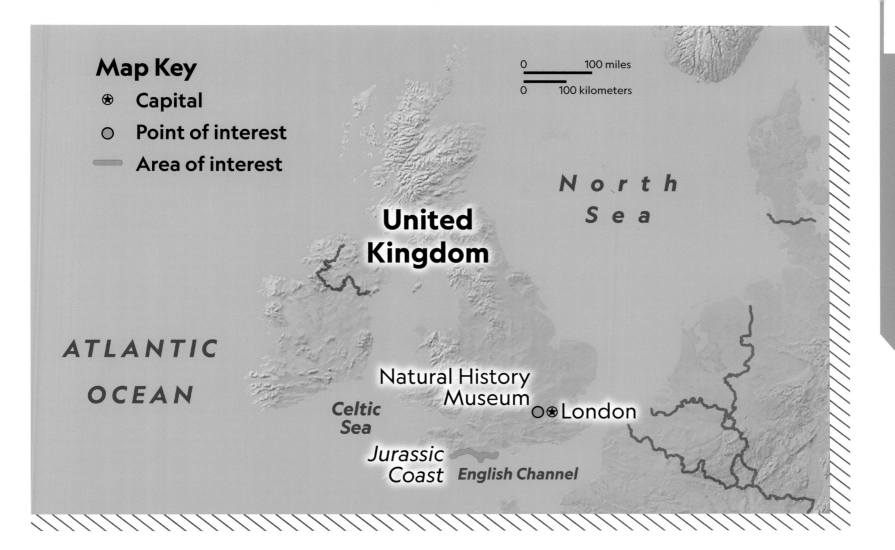

Map Key
⊛ Capital
○ Point of interest
▬ Area of interest

0 ――― 100 miles
0 ――― 100 kilometers

United Kingdom

North Sea

ATLANTIC OCEAN

Natural History Museum

○⊛ London

Celtic Sea

Jurassic Coast *English Channel*

AMMONITES (AM-moh-nites)

MEANING: Named after the ancient Egyptian Ram-God, Amun

PERIOD: Devonian to Late Cretaceous

These ancient cephalopods were like squid with hard shells. Only their shells remain today because their soft bodies did not turn into fossils. Their spiral shells look almost like the curved horns of a ram. They had big heads, large eyes, and tentacles. They fed on phytoplankton and small crustaceans. An ammonite moved by sucking water into its mouth then squirting it out of a tube. This moved the ammonite backward through the water.

SEASHORE DISCOVERIES

Mary Anning looked for fossils as a hobby. In 1823, Anning found the full skeleton of a plesiosaur. In 1828, she found the fossil of the very first pterosaur discovered outside Germany. Even though she had taught herself and had not been taught about geology or ancient history by a teacher, Anning became an expert at finding and collecting fossils. A whole section of the Natural History Museum in London, England, is filled with her finds.

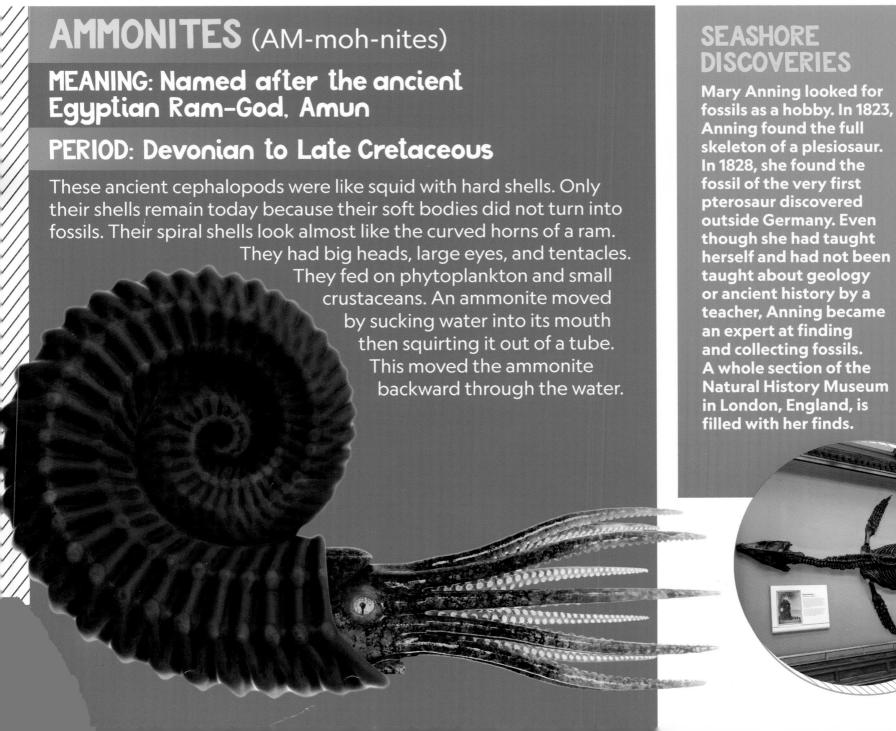

SPOTLIGHT ON:
BAKONYJÁKÓ, HUNGARY

FOSSIL FINDS: *AJKACERATOPS, HUNGAROSAURUS*
WHEN: CRETACEOUS

EUROPE

↑

HUNGARY

During the Late Cretaceous, Hungary was part of a group of islands between Africa and Eurasia in the Tethys Sea. The land was warm with lots of plants, including conifer trees and flowering plants. *Hungarosaurus* and *Ajkaceratops* lived there. So did pterosaurs and crocodilians. Their fossils can now be found in the Csehbánya Formation. It is at a mining site in the Bakony mountains in western Hungary. Scientists think a lot of the fossils here are of animals that got caught in huge floods.

Before *Ajkaceratops* was found in the early 2000s, scientists didn't think ceratopsians lived in Europe in the Late Cretaceous. It took more than 200 years for paleontologists to find a horned dinosaur fossil here!

AJKACERATOPS
(AHJ-ka-SEHR-uh-tops)

MEANING:
"Horn face from Ajka"

PERIOD: Late Cretaceous

Ceratopsians, like *Triceratops*, are usually big. But *Ajkaceratops* was much smaller than horned dinosaurs from other parts of the world in the Late Cretaceous. It was just three feet (1 m) long. That might be because Hungary was an island in the Tethyan Archipelago during the Cretaceous. This meant there was not as much food there as in other places. This could have stopped dinosaurs there from growing very big.

AN UNSOLVED PUZZLE

Europe was a group of islands surrounded by water during the Cretaceous period. Because scientists thought dinosaurs could not swim across this water, they believed European dinosaurs must have been very different from dinosaurs in other places. But the *Ajkaceratops* looked a lot like Asian ceratopsian fossils. This might mean dinosaurs traveled from Asia to Europe during this time. Scientists don't know for sure that this happened, or how it could have happened. Maybe dinosaurs swam across the Tethys Sea. Or maybe they walked across the ocean floor after sea levels dropped.

0 ——— 50 miles
0 ——— 50 kilometers

Budapest

Bakonyjákó ○

Bakony mountains

Hungary

Map Key
⊛ Capital
○ Point of interest

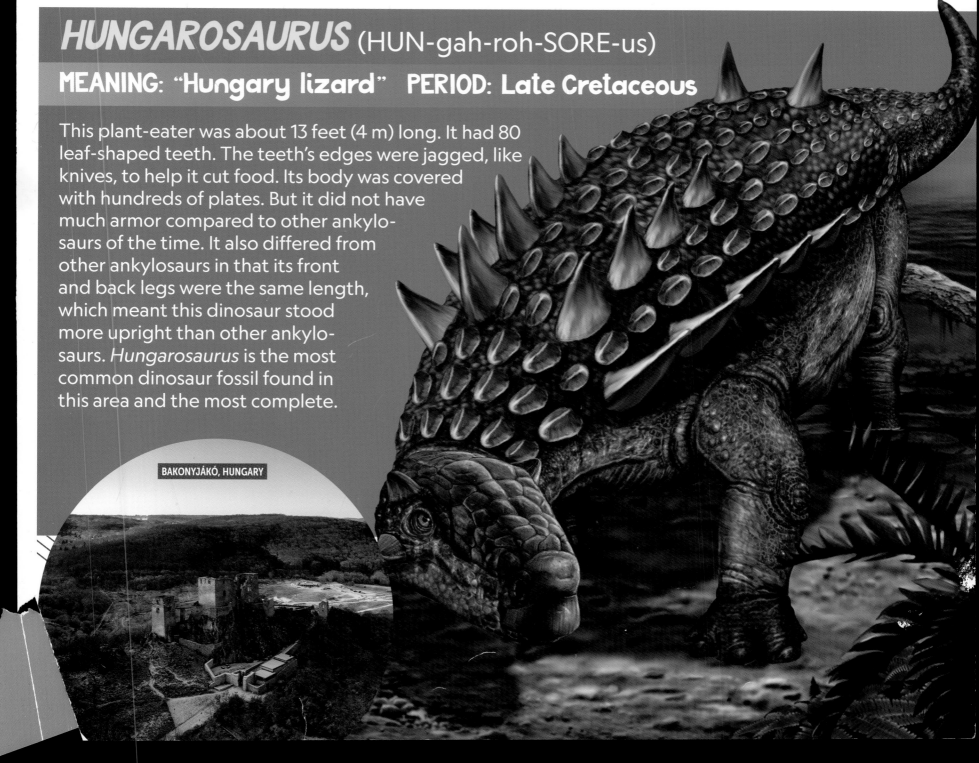

HUNGAROSAURUS (HUN-gah-roh-SORE-us)

MEANING: "Hungary lizard"   PERIOD: Late Cretaceous

This plant-eater was about 13 feet (4 m) long. It had 80 leaf-shaped teeth. The teeth's edges were jagged, like knives, to help it cut food. Its body was covered with hundreds of plates. But it did not have much armor compared to other ankylosaurs of the time. It also differed from other ankylosaurs in that its front and back legs were the same length, which meant this dinosaur stood more upright than other ankylosaurs. *Hungarosaurus* is the most common dinosaur fossil found in this area and the most complete.

BAKONYJÁKÓ, HUNGARY

SPOTLIGHT ON:
BAVARIA, GERMANY

FOSSIL FINDS: *PLATEOSAURUS, ARCHAEOPTERYX*
WHEN: TRIASSIC AND JURASSIC

NEUSCHWANSTEIN CASTLE, GERMANY

EUROPE

↑
GERMANY

People visit Bavaria, Germany, for its green hills and valleys. Tourists often visit its castles. But it is also the site of some big dinosaur finds. Lots of *Plateosaurus* fossils have been found here. During the Triassic and Jurassic periods, Bavaria was a shallow sea with tiny islands that dinosaurs called home. It was much closer to the Equator then, so it was very warm.

PLATEOSAURUS (plat-EE-oh-SORE-us)

MEANING: "Flat lizard" **PERIOD:** Late Triassic

Plateosaurus was one of the largest dinosaurs of its time. It grew to be anywhere from 16 feet (5 m) to 33 feet (10 m) long. It walked on two feet. It had a long, strong tail that helped it balance. *Plateosaurus* used its teeth to crush up plants. Its five fingers included a large thumb claw that might have helped it grab plants and tree branches.

MORE FEATHERED FRIENDS

One of the best preserved fossils ever found in Europe was a meat-eating baby called *Sciurumimus*. It was a theropod from Bavaria. Some of its protofeathers, which are early kinds of feathers, were still there! This species of theropod lived during the Jurassic period 150 million years ago.

ARCHAEOPTERYX FOSSIL

More than 10 *Archaeopteryx* fossils have been found. All of them were from this same place in Germany.

ARCHAEOPTERYX
(ARK-ee-OP-turr-icks)

MEANING: "Ancient wing"

PERIOD: Late Jurassic

Archaeopteryx may be one of the most important fossils ever found. Its bones are like the bones of both dinosaurs and modern birds. That makes it a "transitional fossil." This means that it helped scientists learn how birds and dinosaurs are related. After studying *Archaeopteryx,* scientists figured out that today's birds are dinosaurs. Like other dinosaurs, this early bird had sharp teeth, a bony tail, and three clawed fingers. It also had feathers. Scientists think it could fly—or at least glide after jumping into the air.

North Sea

Baltic Sea

0 — 100 miles
0 — 100 kilometers

Berlin ⊛

Germany

Bavaria

Adriatic Sea

Ligurian Sea

Map Key

⊛ Capital

▢ Area of interest

SPOTLIGHT ON:
AIX-EN-PROVENCE, FRANCE

FOSSIL FINDS: *RHABDODON*, FOSSILIZED EGGS
WHEN: CRETACEOUS

EUROPE

FRANCE

France is one of the countries in Europe with the most dinosaur remains. Dinosaur fossils from all periods of the Mesozoic era have been found at more than 1,000 sites here. Many *Rhabdodon* grazed on the plains of what is now southern France. Fossils from turtles, crocodiles, mammals, and plants have also been found in the country.

MONTAGNE SAINTE-VICTOIRE IS A LIMESTONE MOUNTAIN RIDGE IN THE SOUTH OF FRANCE CLOSE TO AIX-EN-PROVENCE.

RHABDODON
(RAB-doh-don)

MEANING: "Rod tooth"

PERIOD: Late Cretaceous

This 13-foot (4-m)-long ornithopod was the most common dinosaur in Europe during this time. That's why scientists gave it the nickname "Cretaceous cow." *Rhabdodon* teeth were first found in 1869 in southern France. But a more complete skeleton wasn't found in this region until 1995. Another was found in 2007. These fossils helped scientists learn that two different species of *Rhabdodon* lived around southern France and Spain.

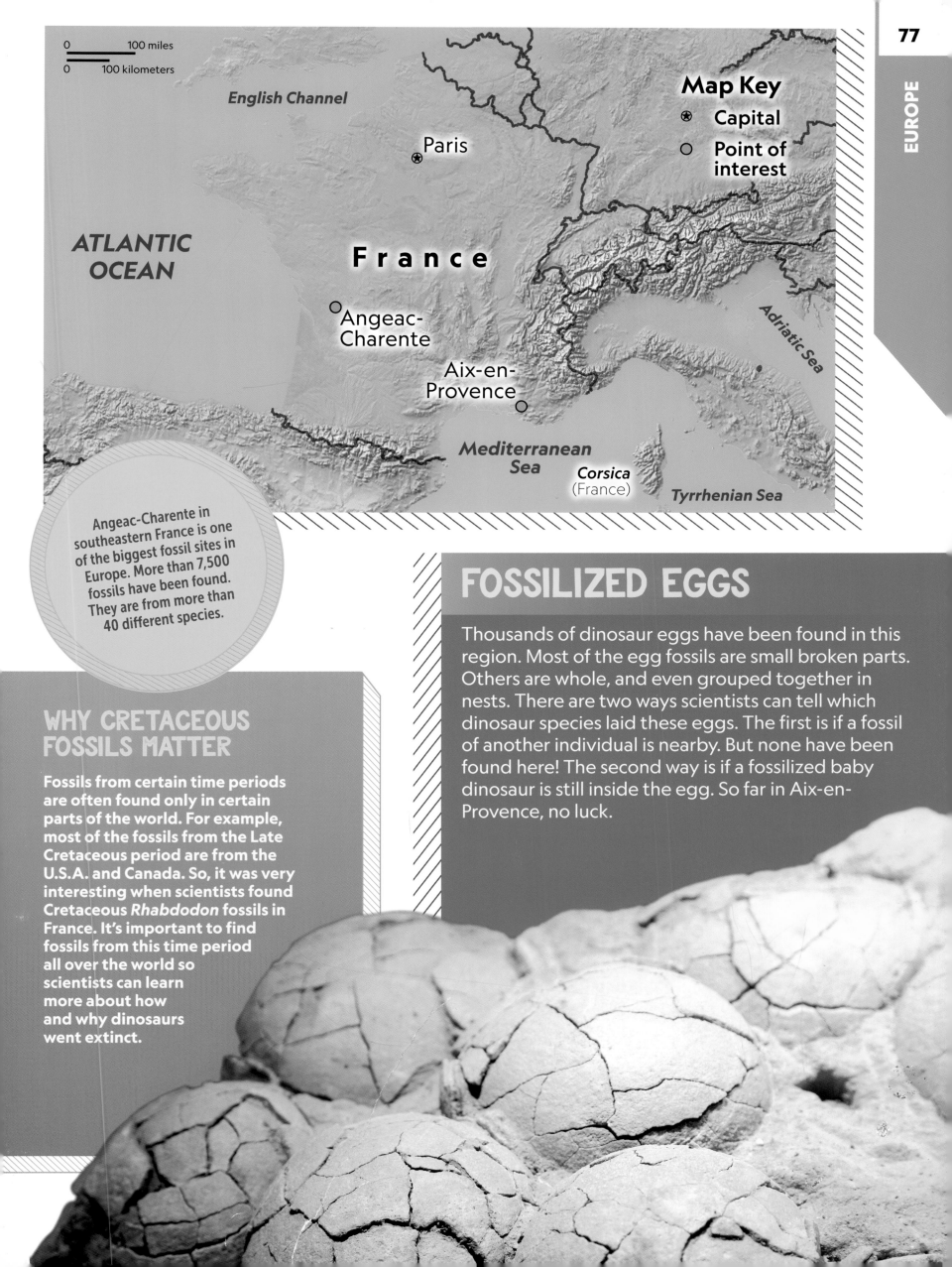

0 100 miles
0 100 kilometers

English Channel

★ Paris

Map Key

⊛ Capital

◯ Point of interest

ATLANTIC OCEAN

F r a n c e

◯ Angeac-Charente

◯ Aix-en-Provence

Adriatic Sea

Mediterranean Sea

Corsica (France)

Tyrrhenian Sea

Angeac-Charente in southeastern France is one of the biggest fossil sites in Europe. More than 7,500 fossils have been found. They are from more than 40 different species.

FOSSILIZED EGGS

Thousands of dinosaur eggs have been found in this region. Most of the egg fossils are small broken parts. Others are whole, and even grouped together in nests. There are two ways scientists can tell which dinosaur species laid these eggs. The first is if a fossil of another individual is nearby. But none have been found here! The second way is if a fossilized baby dinosaur is still inside the egg. So far in Aix-en-Provence, no luck.

WHY CRETACEOUS FOSSILS MATTER

Fossils from certain time periods are often found only in certain parts of the world. For example, most of the fossils from the Late Cretaceous period are from the U.S.A. and Canada. So, it was very interesting when scientists found Cretaceous *Rhabdodon* fossils in France. It's important to find fossils from this time period all over the world so scientists can learn more about how and why dinosaurs went extinct.

AFRICA

Fewer dinosaur fossils have been found in Africa than in some other parts of the world. One reason is that some of the areas—like the harsh Sahara desert environment—can be difficult to explore safely. But paleontologists are beginning to spend much more time searching this important continent. The fossils that have been found here come in all sizes, from dog-size fossils from the mid-Triassic—when the very first dinosaur lived!—all the way to huge titanosaurs from the last days of the Cretaceous.

KALKFELD
NAMIBIA

Two dinosaurs left a track of 170-million-year-old footprints in the soft clay. The trace fossils are from two types of theropods.

OULAD ABDOUN BASIN
MOROCCO

Fossils of *Chenanisaurus*, which had smaller arms and a shorter snout than *T. rex*, were found here. It was one of the last dinosaurs to live in Africa before the Late Cretaceous extinction.

SAHARA
NIGER

A *Nigersaurus* fossil was found here in the very hot desert. This dinosaur had a unique, square-shaped snout. Learn more about it on page 86.

MAIN KAROO BASIN
SOUTH AFRICA

Lots of early land and sea fossils were found in this rock formation. They are from the extinctions at the end of the Permian and Triassic periods.

KEM KEM GROUP
MOROCCO

Theropods like *Spinosaurus,* pterosaurs, birds, turtles, fish, and other marine life from the Late Cretaceous have been found here. Learn more about it on page 80.

SAHARA
EGYPT

A fossil of a *Mansourasaurus*, a school-bus-size sauropod, was found here. Turn to page 81 to learn more about this desert fossil site.

More Dinosaurs of Africa

Aegyptosaurus
(ee-JIP-tuh-SORE-us):
"Egyptian lizard,"
Egypt, Early to
Late Cretaceous

Afrovenator
(af-ro-VEN-ah-tor):
"African hunter,"
Niger, Middle Jurassic

Deltadromeus
(DEL-tah-DROH-mee-us):
"Delta runner,"
Morocco, Egypt,
Late Cretaceous

SOUTH AFRICA

Dinosaur fossils like *Heterodontosaurus* and *Massospondylus* have been found here. So have the fossils of early humans! Learn more on page 84.

MANDA BEDS
TANZANIA

Nyasasaurus may be the oldest dinosaur fossil in the world, and it was found here. Turn to page 83 to learn more.

MOROCCO
Ouled Abdoun Basin
TUNISIA
Mediterranean Sea
Kem Kem group
Western Sahara (Morocco)
ALGERIA
LIBYA
EGYPT
S a h a r a
Red Sea

0   800 miles
0   800 kilometers

CABO VERDE
MAURITANIA
MALI
NIGER
CHAD
SUDAN
ERITREA
SENEGAL
THE GAMBIA →
GUINEA-BISSAU
GUINEA
BURKINA FASO
DJIBOUTI
SIERRA LEONE
LIBERIA
TOGO
BENIN
NIGERIA
GHANA
CÔTE D'IVOIRE (IVORY COAST)
CAMEROON
EQUATORIAL GUINEA →
CENTRAL AFRICAN REPUBLIC
SOUTH SUDAN
ETHIOPIA
SOMALIA
SAO TOME & PRINCIPE
CONGO
GABON
DEMOCRATIC REPUBLIC OF THE CONGO
UGANDA
KENYA
RWANDA
BURUNDI
INDIAN OCEAN
TANZANIA
SEYCHELLES

ATLANTIC OCEAN
Manda Beds
COMOROS
ANGOLA
MALAWI
ZAMBIA
MADAGASCAR
MAURITIUS
ZIMBABWE
Réunion (France)
Kalkfeld
MOZAMBIQUE
NAMIBIA
BOTSWANA
ESWATINI (SWAZILAND)
Main Karoo Basin
LESOTHO
Qhemega
SOUTH AFRICA

QHEMEGA
SOUTH AFRICA

A local herder accidentally found this dinosaur graveyard. Scientists think it may have hundreds of fossils from more than 12 different species of plant-eating sauropodomorphs.

Map Key

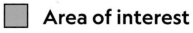 **Point of interest**

Area of interest

The color of each point or area of interest matches its specific caption color on the page.

Kentrosaurus
(KEN-troh-SORE-us):
"Spiky lizard,"
Tanzania,
Late Jurassic

Nqwebasaurus
(n-qu-WEB-ah-SORE-us):
"Nqweba lizard,"
South Africa,
Early Cretaceous

Rugops
(ROO-gops):
"Wrinkle face,"
Niger, Late Cretaceous

SPOTLIGHT ON:
KEM KEM GROUP, MOROCCO AND SAHARA, EGYPT

FOSSIL FINDS: *SPINOSAURUS, MANSOURASAURUS*
WHEN: CRETACEOUS

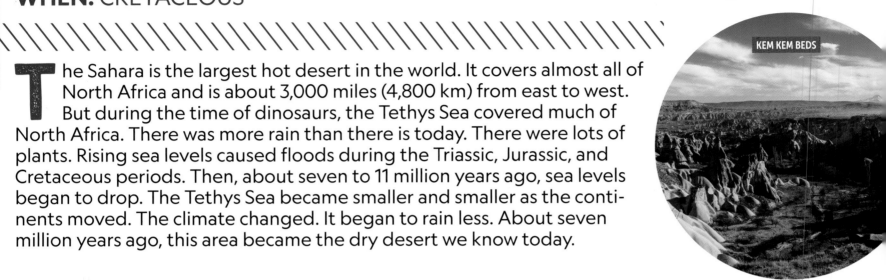

← MOROCCO
← EGYPT

Sahara

AFRICA

KEM KEM BEDS

The Sahara is the largest hot desert in the world. It covers almost all of North Africa and is about 3,000 miles (4,800 km) from east to west. But during the time of dinosaurs, the Tethys Sea covered much of North Africa. There was more rain than there is today. There were lots of plants. Rising sea levels caused floods during the Triassic, Jurassic, and Cretaceous periods. Then, about seven to 11 million years ago, sea levels began to drop. The Tethys Sea became smaller and smaller as the continents moved. The climate changed. It began to rain less. About seven million years ago, this area became the dry desert we know today.

SPINOSAURUS (SPINE-oh-SORE-us)

MEANING: "Spine lizard"   **PERIOD:** Late Cretaceous

There is only one dinosaur known to have swum in water: *Spinosaurus*. Its long crocodile-like snout, long paddle-like tail, and small back legs meant that it could hunt better in water than on land. It used its sharp teeth to snap up large fish. But it is most famous for the six-foot (2-m)-tall "sail" on its back. Scientists believe that at more than 50 feet (15 m) in length, *Spinosaurus* was the largest meat-eater that ever lived.

The only known *Spinosaurus* skeleton in the world was destroyed during World War II. Only drawings and pictures were left—until a new *Spinosaurus* skeleton was found in Morocco in 2013. In 2020, scientists announced that they had found a fossil of a nearly complete *Spinosaurus* tail.

ATLANTIC
OCEAN

Rabat ⊛
○Kem Kem Group
Morocco

Mediterranean Sea

Cairo ⊛

Egypt

S a h a r a

Red Sea

Map Key
⊛ Capital
○ Point of interest
▢ Area of Sahara
   in Egypt

0   400 miles
0   400 kilometers

MANSOURASAURUS
(man-SOUR-uh-SORE-us)

MEANING: "Mansoura lizard"

PERIOD: Late Cretaceous

This sauropod fossil was around the size of a
bus at nearly 33 feet (10 m) long. But that was
small for a titanosaur! This *Mansourasaurus* fossil
found in Egypt may be one of the most complete
dinosaur fossils from the Cretaceous period in Africa.

EXTREME FOSSIL
HUNTING: **The Desert**

In the desert, fossil hunting can get
extreme. Temperatures can get hotter than 100°F (38°C). That much heat
can be dangerous for paleontologists. And
there is almost no shade! The weather can also
bring sudden sandstorms. The winds are strong
enough to blow over a tent. But, luckily, they
also blow away the sands to show new fossils
waiting to be found.

SPOTLIGHT ON:
TANZANIA

FOSSIL FINDS: *GIRAFFATITAN, NYASASAURUS*
WHEN: TRIASSIC AND JURASSIC

AFRICA

TANZANIA ➔

Today, Tanzania is a popular place to visit. Serengeti National Park and Kilimanjaro National Park are here. The country is a great place to see lions, leopards, elephants, buffalo, and rhinoceroses. It's also home to some important fossil sites. Two are in southern Tanzania: the Tendaguru Formation and Lake Nyasa.

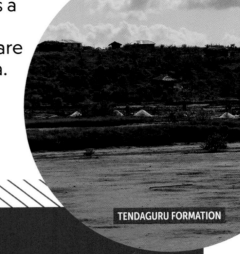

TENDAGURU FORMATION

GIRAFFATITAN (ji-RAF-a-TIE-tan)

MEANING: "Giant giraffe"   **PERIOD:** Late Jurassic

Between 1909 and 1913, more than 225 tons (204 t) of dinosaur bones were found in Tendaguru. This included a group of *Giraffatitans*. Scientists think these long-necked dinosaurs may have died after getting stuck in the mud near a Jurassic lagoon. When these fossils were first found, scientists thought they might belong to an African species of *Brachiosaurus*. This is because the fossils are very long, at around 75 feet (23 m). But now scientists know *Giraffatitan* was a different species.

You can see Oskar, a 43-foot (13-m)-tall *Giraffatitan* fossil, at the Museum für Naturkunde in Berlin, Germany. It holds the world record for the tallest dinosaur skeleton on display.

0 ——— 200 miles
0 ——— 200 kilometers

Lake Victoria

Lake Tanganyika

Dodoma ⊛

Tanzania   Dar es ⊛ Salaam

Tendaguru Formation ○

INDIAN OCEAN

Manda Beds ○

Lake Nyasa (Lake Malawi)

Map Key

⊛ Capital

○ Point of interest

ONLY TIME WILL TELL

Though the *Nyasasaurus* bones were found in the 1930s, it took scientists about 80 years to study them! Why did it take them that long? Sometimes it takes years to find the people and money needed to take a fossil safely from the ground. Then once it's in a laboratory, it can take months or years for experts (or volunteers!) to clean the fossil.

Scientists think that many dinosaurs may have used their tails for balance ... or as weapons!

NYASASAURUS
(ny-AS-ah-SORE-us)

MEANING: "Lizard of Lake Nyasa"

PERIOD: Middle Triassic

This 7-to-10-foot (2–3 m)-long archosaur was a plant-eater. It had a long neck and tail, and it walked on two legs. In fact, the *Nyasasaurus* may have been the first dinosaur to walk the planet, more than 240 million years ago. Scientists used to think *Eoraptor* was the oldest dinosaur, but *Nyasasaurus* is millions of years older! The bones were found in the Manda Beds near Lake Nyasa in the 1930s.

SPOTLIGHT ON:
SOUTH AFRICA

FOSSIL FINDS: *HETERODONTOSAURUS, MASSOSPONDYLUS*
WHEN: JURASSIC

AFRICA

SOUTH
AFRICA

Today, South Africa has lots of mountains. In the Early Jurassic, it was flat and dry, but there were lots of streams. Important dinosaur fossils have been found here. It's also the site of another important kind of fossil: early humans! Humans, early humans, and their relatives are called hominins. Lots of kinds of hominin fossils have been found in South Africa. Some hominin fossils from South Africa are more than three million years old.

SOUTH AFRICA

HUMAN RELATIVES

Just as dinosaurs are related to each other, different kinds of hominins—including modern humans like us—are related. In 2013, paleontologist Lee Berger led a team to explore a group of caves in South Africa. There, they found a hominin who lived about 236,000 to 335,000 years ago! This kind of hominin, now called *Homo naledi,* was a new human relative who had never been found before. Scientists are studying *Homo naledi* to learn more about how early hominins became the humans we are today.

HETERODONTOSAURUS
(HET-er-oh-DAHNT-oh-SORE-us)

MEANING: "Different teeth lizard"

PERIOD: Early Jurassic

The four-foot (1.2-m)-long *Heterodontosaurus* had three different kinds of teeth. It had small teeth shaped like triangles, longer teeth like tusks, and square teeth for chomping. Scientists used to think the tusk-like teeth didn't grow until the dinosaur was a teenager. They also thought *Heterodontosaurus* ate only plants. But a two-inch (5-cm)-long baby skull showed they were wrong. The skull had tusk-like teeth! Now scientists think the tusks helped keep *Heterodontosaurus* safe or helped it hunt. They also think it may have been an omnivore—not a herbivore.

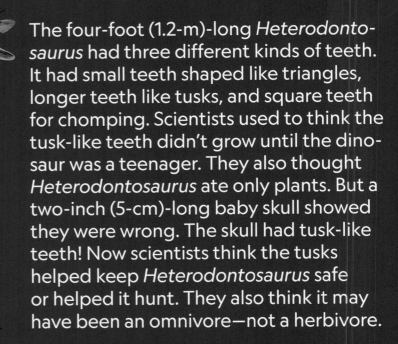

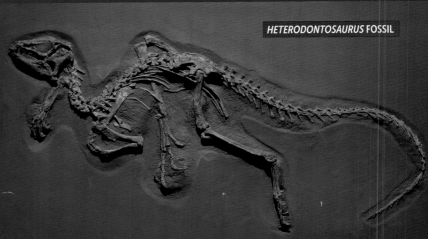

HETERODONTOSAURUS FOSSIL

Map Key

⊛ Capital

○ Point of interest

▢ Area of interest

ATLANTIC OCEAN

Pretoria (Tshwane)

Golden Gate Highlands National Park

Bloemfontein

South Africa

Main Karoo Basin

Cape Town

INDIAN OCEAN

0 — 200 miles
0 — 200 kilometers

DINOSAUR NESTING GROUND

In 1976 in South Africa's Golden Gate Highlands National Park, eggs were found with baby *Massospondylus* fossils inside. In 2006, paleontologists found 10 more groups of eggs. One group had at least 34 eggs! *Massospondylus* mothers raised babies here about 200 million years ago. That makes it the oldest known site where dinosaurs nested in groups. Back then, this area was near a lake. When it flooded, the eggs were covered with sediment and became fossils.

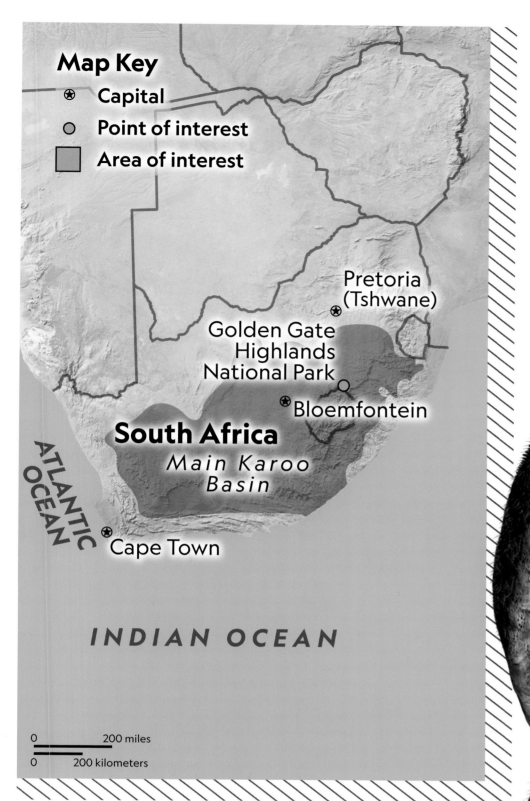

Ledumahadi mafube was also found in South Africa. It's a four-legged sauropod that weighed as much as two large African elephants.

MASSOSPONDYLUS
(MASS-oh-SPON-dih-lus)

MEANING: "Huge vertebrae"

PERIOD: Early Jurassic

Massospondylus fossils are a fairly common find in South Africa, including fossils from dinos of different ages. The adult *Massospondylus* fossils have longer back legs than their front limbs. But the fossils of the young had legs all about the same size. This helped scientists learn that baby *Massospondylus* walked on four legs, but adults walked on two. Adult *Massospondylus* were 13 feet (4 m) long. They had five fingers and clawed thumbs, which may mean they ate both plants and meat. Fingers would help them grab plants, and claws would help them hunt.

SPOTLIGHT ON:
SAHARA, NIGER

FOSSIL FINDS: *NIGERSAURUS, JOBARIA*
WHEN: JURASSIC AND CRETACEOUS

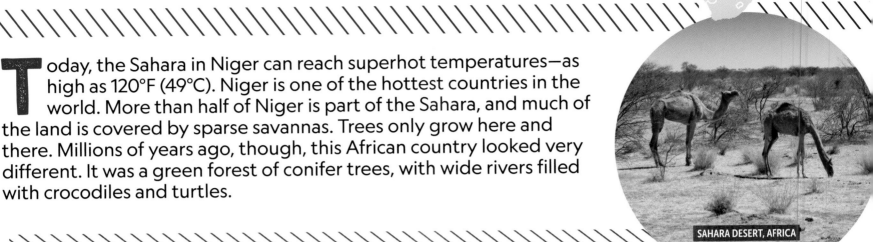

Sahara

NIGER

AFRICA

Today, the Sahara in Niger can reach superhot temperatures—as high as 120°F (49°C). Niger is one of the hottest countries in the world. More than half of Niger is part of the Sahara, and much of the land is covered by sparse savannas. Trees only grow here and there. Millions of years ago, though, this African country looked very different. It was a green forest of conifer trees, with wide rivers filled with crocodiles and turtles.

SAHARA DESERT, AFRICA

NIGERSAURUS (NYE-jer-SORE-us)

MEANING: "Niger lizard"   **PERIOD:** Early Cretaceous

This elephant-size herbivore had a snout shaped like a square that grew at an angle instead of straight forward. This let *Nigersaurus* eat ferns off the ground like a cow does—or like a vacuum cleaner! If this dinosaur ever broke a tooth, a new one would replace it. Each tooth had nine others below it. And there were 50 rows of teeth. This means *Nigersaurus* had about 600 teeth over its lifetime!

NIGERSAURUS SKULL

MADE-UP MONSTER ▶

The Tuareg people are a nomadic tribe, meaning they do not live in one place. They travel across the Sahara on camels. For many years, they told stories of a giant creature called Jobar. The stories were inspired by the huge bones they saw while they traveled through the desert. When American paleontologist Paul Sereno came looking for fossils, a Tuareg guide helped him by showing him "Jobar's graveyard"—the place where the bones from the stories were. It was a dinosaur fossil! Sereno named the new dinosaur species *Jobaria*, after the stories.

ATLANTIC
OCEAN

Mediterranean Sea

Map Key

★ Capital

○ Point of
   interest

▢ Area of
   Sahara
   in Niger

S a h a r a

Niger

○*Jobar's
graveyard*

Red Sea

Niamey ⊛

0 ⊢ 400 miles
0 ⊢ 400 kilometers

Many fossils of all kinds
have been found in a part
of this desert in Tunisia,
including the jaw of a
giant crocodilian,
Sarcosuchus, about
110 million years old.

JOBARIA
(joh-BAR-ee-uh)

MEANING:
Named after the
Tuareg mythical
creature, Jobar

PERIOD: Middle Jurassic

Jobaria was a 30-foot (9-m)-tall, 70-foot (21-m)-
long sauropod. Scientists found seven *Jobaria* fossils
in the 1990s. They think the dinosaurs died during a
flood because they found some fossils on top of
others. When *Jobaria* was first found, scientists
believed it was from the Cretaceous. But *Jobaria*'s
neck and tail were much shorter than those of
other sauropods from the Cretaceous. And its
body was bigger. It weighed as much as four
African elephants! Now scientists
think *Jobaria* was from the
Middle Jurassic. So it
makes sense that
it was different
from Cretaceous
sauropods.

JOBARIA
FOSSIL

ASIA

More dinosaur fossils have been found in Asia over the past few decades than on any other continent. During the Mesozoic era, the Asian deserts, plains, and mountains of today were covered in plants and swamps. As the land shifted, lakes and mountain ranges formed across East Asia. Dinosaurs roamed the region. Today, dry deserts and rocky mountains keep their fossils safe. More and more people are looking for fossils in Asia—and finding them!

RAHIOLI
INDIA

The Balasinor Dinosaur Fossil Park in Rahioli is one of the most important sites for dinosaur fossils in India. Learn about the *Rajasaurus* and more on page 94.

ZHUCHENG
CHINA

More than 7,000 fossils from the Late Cretaceous have been found here, including ceratopsians, ankylosaurs, and hadrosaurs.

KALASIN PROVINCE
THAILAND

A trackway of 21 dinosaur footprints was uncovered here beginning in 1996 in the Phu Faek Forest Park.

KYZYLKUM DESERT
UZBEKISTAN

In 2021, scientists announced an astonishing find: a predator five times the size of a tyrannosaur! *Ulughbegsaurus* (oo-LOOG-bek-SAW-rus), which lived alongside early tyrannosaurs, likely prevented them from becoming the apex predators we know them to be today. When *Ulughbegsaurus* went extinct 90 million years ago, tyrannosaurs finally got their chance to shine.

JABALPUR
INDIA

The first recorded dinosaur fossils found in Asia, vertebrae from a sauropod, were found near here in 1828.

PHU WIANG
THAILAND

The fossils of meat-eating dinosaurs called *Phuwiangvenator* were found here. These predators ran on two legs.

GOBI DESERT
MONGOLIA

Many of the best dinosaur skeletons, including *Velociraptor*, were found in this desert. Learn more on page 90.

More Dinosaurs of Asia

Achillobator
(ah-kill-oh-BATE-or):
"Achilles hero,"
Mongolia,
Late Cretaceous

Psittacosaurus
(SIT-ah-coh-SORE-us):
"Parrot lizard,"
China, Mongolia,
Russia, Early Cretaceous

Barapasaurus
(BAH-rap-oh-SORE-us):
"Big leg lizard,"
India, Early Jurassic

LIAONING
CHINA

Paleontologists found fossils of lots of Early Cretaceous animals well preserved here, including feathered dinosaurs like *Microraptor*. Turn to page 92 for more.

FUKUI
JAPAN

Lots of the fossils found in Japan—including *Fukuiraptor*, a large theropod from the Early Cretaceous—have been found here.

ARCTIC OCEAN

0 — 600 miles
0 — 600 kilometers

RUSSIA

TURKEY
GEORGIA
ARMENIA
AZERBAIJAN
LEBANON
SYRIA
EGYPT ISRAEL
JORDAN
IRAQ
KAZAKHSTAN
UZBEKISTAN
Kyzylkum Desert
TURKMENISTAN
KYRGYZSTAN
TAJIKISTAN
SAUDI ARABIA
KUWAIT
IRAN
AFGHANISTAN
BAHRAIN →
QATAR
UNITED ARAB EMIRATES
PAKISTAN
YEMEN
OMAN
Arabian Sea

MONGOLIA
Gobi Desert
Liaoning
NORTH KOREA
SOUTH KOREA
Zhucheng
CHINA
JAPAN
Fukui
PACIFIC OCEAN

Mediterranean Sea

NEPAL
BHUTAN
Rahioli
Jabalpur
BANGLADESH
INDIA
MYANMAR (BURMA)
LAOS
Phu Wiang
Kalasin
THAILAND
VIETNAM
CAMBODIA
Bay of Bengal

TAIWAN

PHILIPPINES

South China Sea

SRI LANKA

BRUNEI

MALAYSIA

INDONESIA

SINGAPORE
Java Sea
TIMOR-LESTE

INDIAN OCEAN

Map Key

● **Point of interest**

■ **Area of interest**

The color of each point or area of interest matches its specific caption color on the page.

Tsintaosaurus
(sin-tau-SORE-us):
"Qingdao lizard,"
China, Late Cretaceous

Talarurus
(TAL-a-RUR-us):
"Wicker tail,"
Mongolia,
Late Cretaceous

Omeisaurus
(OH-may-SORE-us):
"Omei lizard,"
China, Middle Jurassic

SPOTLIGHT ON:
GOBI DESERT, MONGOLIA

FOSSIL FINDS: *VELOCIRAPTOR, OVIRAPTOR*
WHEN: CRETACEOUS

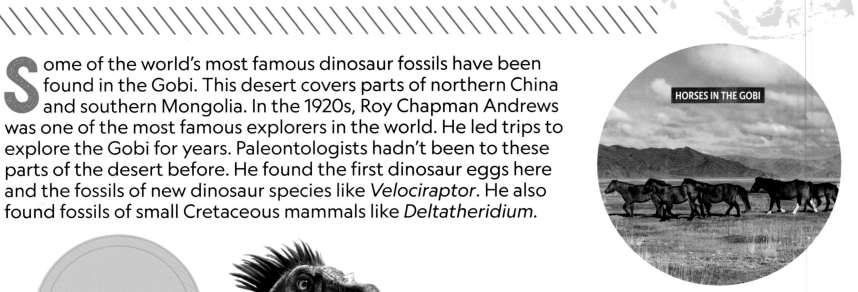

MONGOLIA

ASIA

CHINA

Gobi Desert

TAIWAN

Some of the world's most famous dinosaur fossils have been found in the Gobi. This desert covers parts of northern China and southern Mongolia. In the 1920s, Roy Chapman Andrews was one of the most famous explorers in the world. He led trips to explore the Gobi for years. Paleontologists hadn't been to these parts of the desert before. He found the first dinosaur eggs here and the fossils of new dinosaur species like *Velociraptor*. He also found fossils of small Cretaceous mammals like *Deltatheridium*.

HORSES IN THE GOBI

The Gobi has more than 60 known fossil sites.

VELOCIRAPTOR CLAW

VELOCIRAPTOR
(vel-OSS-ih-RAP-tor)

MEANING: "Quick thief"

PERIOD: Late Cretaceous

In some movies, *Velociraptors* look as big as a person. In real life, they were actually pretty small—about the size of a turkey. And they had feathers. They ate other small dinosaurs (like *Protoceratops*) with their sharp, pointy teeth. They hunted their prey using a curved, three-inch (8-cm)-long claw on each back foot.

DINO DISCOVERER:
Bolortsetseg (Bolor) Minjin

Bolor is a Mongolian paleontologist and National Geographic Explorer. She founded the Institute for the Study of Mongolian Dinosaurs. The institute discovers new fossil species and trains new paleontologists. Bolor is also working on a new Gobi Dinosaur Museum at the site of the first dino egg nest discovery. Bolor's work also involves adventure: Once she helped stop an illegal sale of a dinosaur skeleton found in Mongolia. For her bravery, Minjin received an award from the Mongolian government called the Order of the Polar Star.

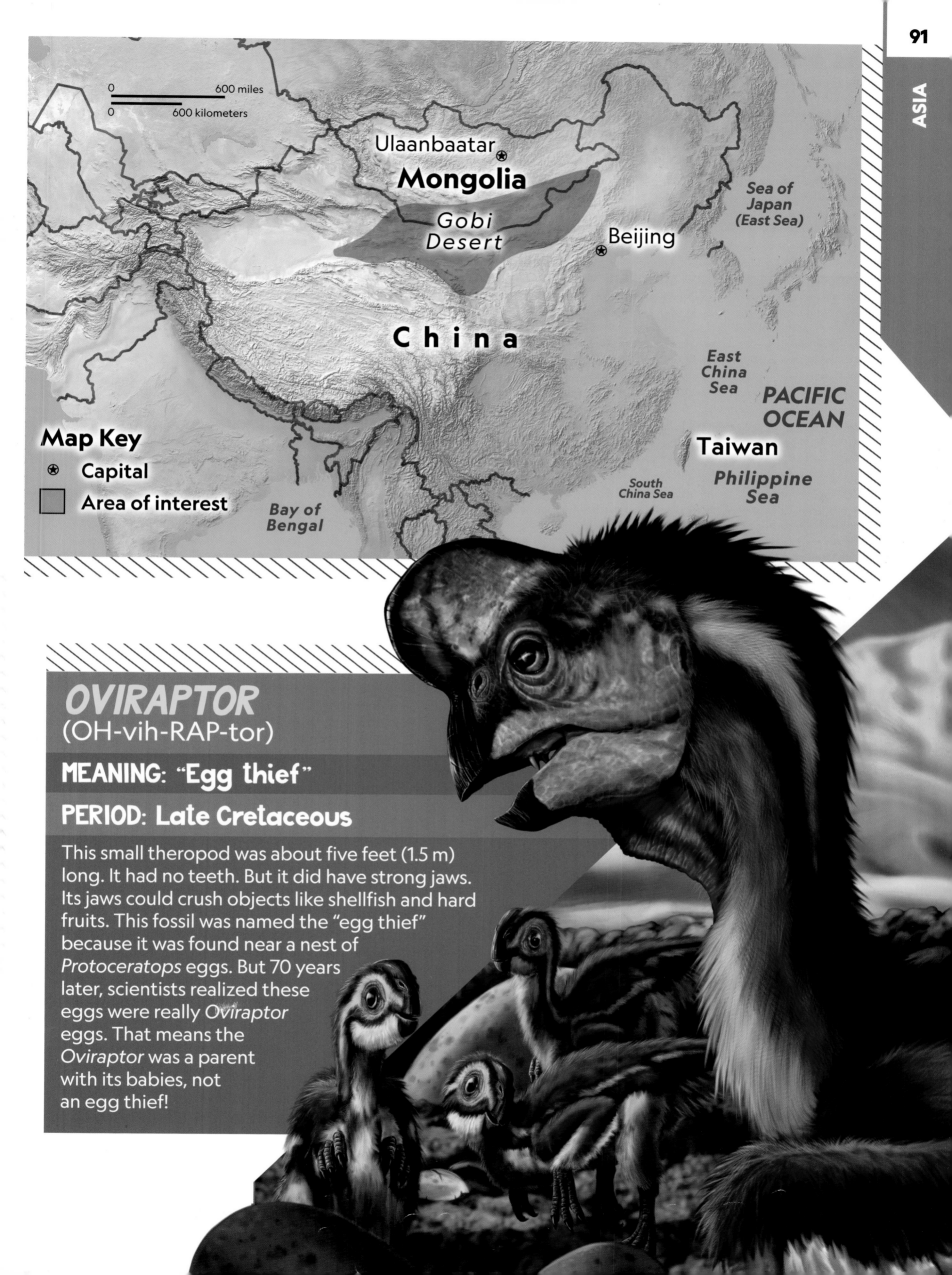

0 600 miles
0 600 kilometers

Ulaanbaatar
Mongolia
Gobi Desert

Beijing

C h i n a

Sea of Japan (East Sea)

East China Sea

PACIFIC OCEAN

Taiwan

Philippine Sea

South China Sea

Bay of Bengal

Map Key
⊛ Capital
▦ Area of interest

OVIRAPTOR
(OH-vih-RAP-tor)

MEANING: "Egg thief"

PERIOD: Late Cretaceous

This small theropod was about five feet (1.5 m) long. It had no teeth. But it did have strong jaws. Its jaws could crush objects like shellfish and hard fruits. This fossil was named the "egg thief" because it was found near a nest of *Protoceratops* eggs. But 70 years later, scientists realized these eggs were really *Oviraptor* eggs. That means the *Oviraptor* was a parent with its babies, not an egg thief!

SPOTLIGHT ON:
LIAONING, CHINA

FOSSIL FINDS: *SINOSAUROPTERYX, MICRORAPTOR*
WHEN: CRETACEOUS

BATA MOUNTAIN, LIAONING PROVINCE, CHINA

A S I A
CHINA
TAIWAN

During the Cretaceous period, Liaoning was full of forests and shallow lakes. The weather was mild. Then, about 125 million years ago, lots of dinosaurs died after volcanoes erupted in northern China. These eruptions helped bury their bodies right away, protecting their bones as they turned into fossils. In fact, scientists found melanosomes in their fossils. Melanosomes are tiny bits of the body that give animals their colors. They are so small you need a microscope to see them. By looking at these melanosomes, scientists could tell what color the dinosaurs' feathers might have been. This had never been done before!

SINOSAUROPTERYX
(SINE-oh-SORE-op-TEHR-iks)

MEANING: "Chinese lizard wing"

PERIOD: Early Cretaceous

Scientists think *Sinosauropteryx* did not use its feathers to fly. Instead, the feathers may have kept it warm, attracted mates, or frightened away other animals. Scientists also believe this dinosaur had light and dark striped feathers along its tail. When they looked at the melanosomes, they learned the feathers may have been orange and white. Before the first *Sinosauropteryx* fossil was found in 1996, scientists didn't know if dinosaurs really had feathers. Now, more than 1,000 fossils of feathered dinosaurs have been found in China.

Today, modern birds get a lot of their colors from melanosomes. But many birds also get their colors from the foods they eat. One example is flamingos. These birds get their bright pink color from eating lots of tiny pink shrimp.

SINOSAUROPTERYX FOSSIL

DINO DISCOVERER: Xu Xing

Microraptor was announced in 2003 by paleontologist Xu Xing. He has found more than 60 fossils in China. He has named more dinosaurs than any other paleontologist alive. That's how he's earned the nickname "China's dinosaur king." He spends his summers looking for fossils in western China.

MICRORAPTOR
(MIKE-row-RAP-tor)

MEANING: "Tiny thief"

PERIOD: Early Cretaceous

This relative of *Velociraptor* was 2.5 feet (0.8 m) long and had feathers. Scientists who studied its melanosomes think it was a shiny dark color, like a crow. But unlike a crow, it had four wings instead of two. It may have used its wings to fly and glide down from trees. *Microraptor* dined on other small animals like insects, fish, and lizards.

0 | 600 miles
0 | 600 kilometers

Sea of Japan (East Sea)

Liaoning

Beijing ✪

China

East China Sea

PACIFIC OCEAN

Taiwan

Philippine Sea

Map Key

⊛ Capital

☐ Area of interest

Bay of Bengal

South China Sea

SPOTLIGHT ON:
RAHIOLI, GUJARAT, INDIA
FOSSIL FINDS: *MEGALOOLITHUS, RAJASAURUS*
WHEN: CRETACEOUS

ASIA

INDIA

In the 1980s, geologists were studying the rocks in Rahioli, India. There, they found stones the size of grapefruits. They were dinosaur eggs! This part of western India is the best place in the country to find dinosaur fossils. Now some of this area is a park protected by the government. Parts of fossils of different species have been found here. So have thousands of dinosaur eggs. Scientists think the thick plants and soft soil in the area were perfect for hatching and protecting them.

"DINOSAUR PRINCESS" AALIYA SULTANA BABI POSES WITH A FOSSIL AT THE BALASINOR DINOSAUR FOSSIL PARK AT RAHIOLI, LOCATED SOME 60 MILES (100 KM) FROM AHMEDABAD.

MEGALOOLITHUS (MEG-ah-LOO-lih-thus)

MEANING: "Large egg stone"

PERIOD: Late Cretaceous

All dinosaur eggs are put into the oospecies category. Thousands of a type of oospecies, called *Megaloolithus* for their size, have been found in this region of India. One of these finds was a 67-million-year-old nest of three eggs. One of these egg fossils was very surprising to scientists. It contained a newly hatched 1.5-foot (0.5-m)-long titanosaur. And the egg held another surprise: A 10-foot (3-m)-long snake fossil (*Sanajeh indicus*) was wrapped around it!

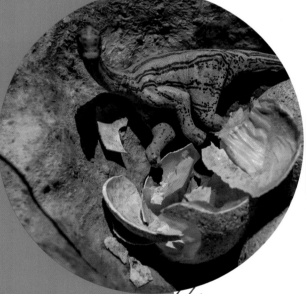

KEEPING FOSSILS SAFE

Balasinor Dinosaur Fossil Park is protected by the government. But that doesn't stop some people from poaching, or stealing, the fossils. They often do this to sell them and make money. When fossils are stolen, it means that scientists can't study them. Every fossil is important for scientists. What if it's the only dinosaur fossil in the world that exists from that species? By keeping fossils safe, paleontologists are protecting history.

Map Key

⊛ Capital

○ Point of interest

0 ——— 400 miles

0 ——— 400 kilometers

New
Delhi ⊛

I n d i a

Balasinor ○
Dinosaur
Park,
Rahioli

Indian ○
Museum,
Kolkāta

*Arabian
Sea*

*Bay of
Bengal*

*Andaman
Islands*

*Andaman
Sea*

INDIAN OCEAN

Princess Aaliya Sultana
Babi is known as the
"Dinosaur Princess" because
she helps make sure fossils
are protected and gives
tours at Balasinor
Dinosaur Fossil Park.

RAJASAURUS (RAH-zha-SORE-us)

MEANING: "King lizard"

PERIOD: Late Cretaceous

This 30-foot (9-m)-long predator ate other dinosaurs for lunch, including long-necked sauropods.
Rajasaurus was the first dinosaur skull found in
India. It had broken into pieces, so it had to be
put back together carefully. *Rajasaurus* had
an unusual bone on its skull that may have
been a horn. The fossil was found in 1983,
but it took paleontologists until 2003
to announce their findings. The skull
is now on display at the Indian
Museum in Kolkāta.

SPOTLIGHT ON:
PHU WIANG NATIONAL PARK, THAILAND

ASIA

←THAILAND

FOSSIL FINDS: *SIRINDHORNA, PHUWIANGOSAURUS*
WHEN: CRETACEOUS

In 1976, Thailand's first dinosaur fossil was found—by accident! Geologists were searching the area for a metal called uranium when they came across a fossilized dinosaur knee bone. The place where it was found, Phu Wiang National Park, is now known as one of the world's biggest dinosaur graveyards.

Paleontologists have found fossils of many animals—from theropods to small crocodiles to mussels—in the Phu Wiang mountains. During the time of the dinosaurs, this northeastern part of Thailand was full of giant trees. A big group of rivers split the area into islands. Then, later in the Cretaceous period, it became a desert.

A PALEONTOLOGIST CLEANS A FOSSIL IN PHU WIANG NATIONAL PARK.

SIRINDHORNA (SEER-en-TORN-uh)

MEANING: Named for Princess Maha Chakri Sirindhorn

PERIOD: Early Cretaceous

In 2007, a fossil similar to an *Iguanodon* was found. It had a long beak-like jaw and a sharp point on each foot. Scientists named it *Sirindhorna khoratensis* to honor Thailand's Princess Maha Chakri Sirindhorn, who had supported the creation of the country's first dinosaur museum. *Sirindhorna* weighed one ton (0.9 t), and was 20 feet (6 m) long and about 6.5 feet (2 m) tall.

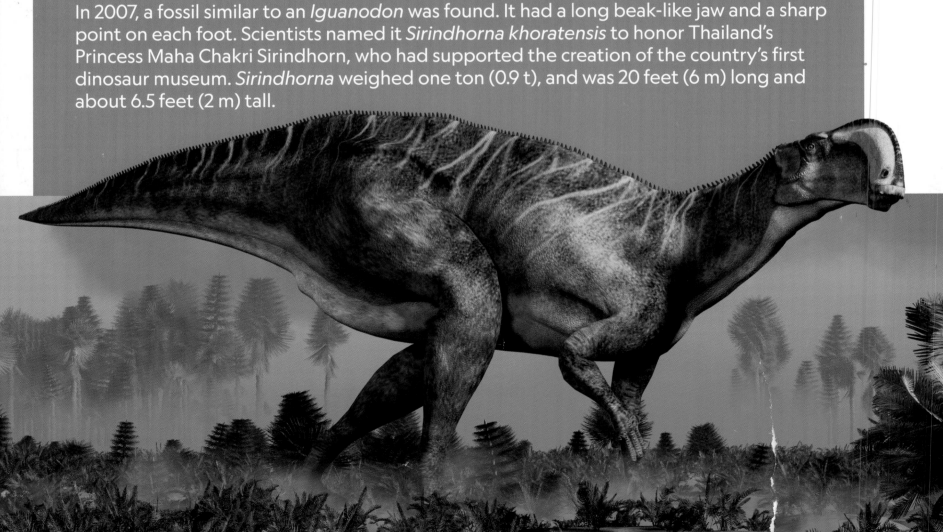

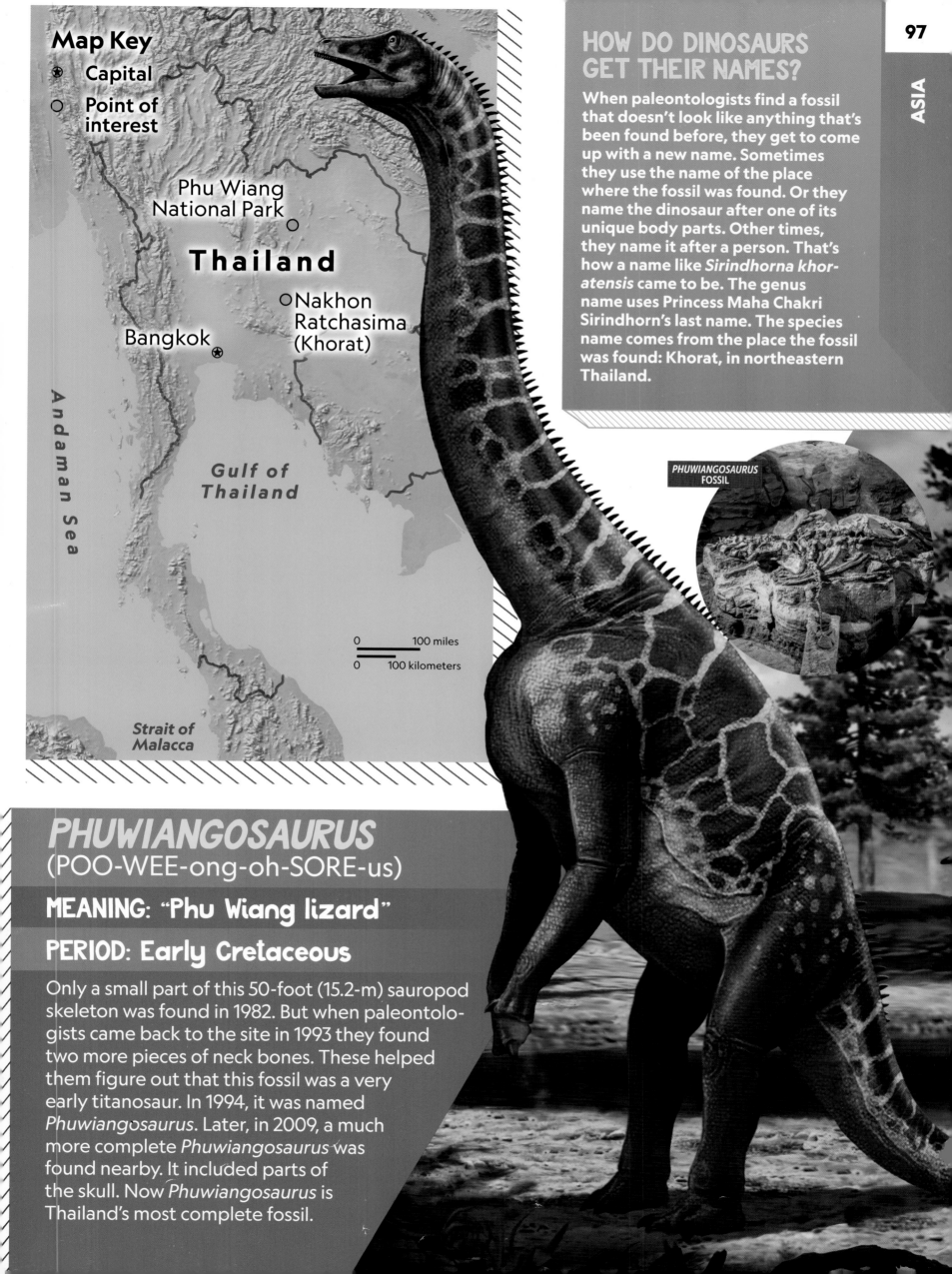

Map Key

★ Capital
○ Point of interest

Phu Wiang
National Park ○

Thailand

○ Nakhon
Ratchasima
(Khorat)

Bangkok ★

Andaman Sea

Gulf of
Thailand

0 ——— 100 miles
0 ——— 100 kilometers

Strait of
Malacca

HOW DO DINOSAURS GET THEIR NAMES?

When paleontologists find a fossil that doesn't look like anything that's been found before, they get to come up with a new name. Sometimes they use the name of the place where the fossil was found. Or they name the dinosaur after one of its unique body parts. Other times, they name it after a person. That's how a name like *Sirindhorna khoratensis* came to be. The genus name uses Princess Maha Chakri Sirindhorn's last name. The species name comes from the place the fossil was found: Khorat, in northeastern Thailand.

PHUWIANGOSAURUS
FOSSIL

PHUWIANGOSAURUS
(POO-WEE-ong-oh-SORE-us)

MEANING: "Phu Wiang lizard"

PERIOD: Early Cretaceous

Only a small part of this 50-foot (15.2-m) sauropod skeleton was found in 1982. But when paleontologists came back to the site in 1993 they found two more pieces of neck bones. These helped them figure out that this fossil was a very early titanosaur. In 1994, it was named *Phuwiangosaurus*. Later, in 2009, a much more complete *Phuwiangosaurus* was found nearby. It included parts of the skull. Now *Phuwiangosaurus* is Thailand's most complete fossil.

AUSTRALIA, NEW ZEALAND, AND ANTARCTICA

Once Pangaea started to split about 200 million years ago, one part moved north. Another part moved south and became Gondwana. This supercontinent was made up of Australia, New Zealand, and Antarctica, as well as South America, India, and Africa. But then, about 180 million years ago, Gondwana started to break up. Australia moved closer to the Arctic Circle. That means what is now southern Australia was home to dinosaurs that lived through long, dark winters that were colder than other places on the planet. During the Cretaceous period, a valley of forests formed between Australia and Antarctica.

HAWKE BAY
NEW ZEALAND

In the early 1970s, the first known dinosaur fossil in New Zealand was found here by a fossil hunter named Joan Wiffen.

GANTHEAUME POINT
AUSTRALIA

When the tide is low on this rocky beach, people can see 130-million-year-old footprints from a three-toed carnivore. Sometimes, they can only be seen for an hour each day.

QUEENSLAND
AUSTRALIA

Wintonotitan, a titanosaur, and *Australovenator*, a *mega-raptor*, were found in the Cretaceous period rocks of the Winton Formation. Turn to page 102 to learn more.

NEW SOUTH WALES
AUSTRALIA

In 1984, about 60 dinosaur bones were found outside the town of Lightning Ridge. They were extra special because they were made of the glittering gemstone opal!

LARK QUARRY
AUSTRALIA

More than 3,000 dinosaur footprints have been found here. They were made by chicken-size coelurosaurs and slightly larger ornithopods about 95 million years ago. The tracks may have been made during a stampede.

VICTORIA
AUSTRALIA

The coast of Australia used to be a valley between Antarctica and Australia. In Gippsland, Victoria, *Galleonosaurus* and other fossils have been found. Turn to page 100 to learn more.

More Dinosaurs of Australia, New Zealand, and Antarctica

Austrosaurus
(OSS-trah-SORE-us):
"Southern lizard,"
Australia,
Early Cretaceous

Diamantinasaurus
(DIE-uh-mun-TEE-nuh-SORE-us):
"Diamantina [River] lizard,"
Australia, Late Cretaceous

Glacialisaurus
(GLAY-shull-ih-SORE-us):
"Icy lizard," Antarctica,
Early Jurassic

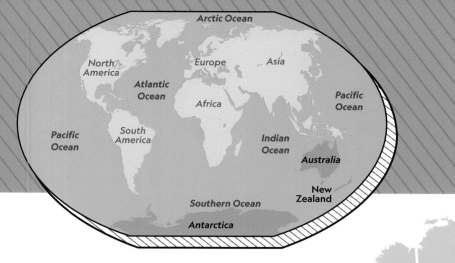

Arctic Ocean

North America • Europe • Asia

Atlantic Ocean

Pacific Ocean • Africa • Indian Ocean

South America • Australia

Southern Ocean • New Zealand

Antarctica

Scientists don't know exactly what many of the fossils found in New Zealand are. That's because for many of the skeletons, only parts have been found.

Gantheaume Point

Lark Quarry Conservation Park

Queensland

AUSTRALIA

New South Wales

Victoria

Gippsland

PACIFIC OCEAN

Map Key

● Point of interest

▪ Area of interest

The color of each point or area of interest matches its specific caption color on the page.

0 — 600 miles

0 — 600 kilometers

INDIAN OCEAN

NEW ZEALAND

Hawke Bay

Cook Strait

COOK STRAIT
NEW ZEALAND

Tens of thousands of reptiles called tuatara live in this area today. They are part of the sphenodontid group, which also includes ancient reptiles that lived at the time of the dinosaurs. Tuatara are the only sphenodontids alive today.

SOUTHERN OCEAN

Wilkes Land

Ridge A
East Antarctica

Polar Plateau

ANTARCTICA

West Antarctica

Queen Maud Land

Antarctic Circle

SOUTHERN OCEAN

James Ross Island

JAMES ROSS ISLAND
ANTARCTICA

It's not easy to find fossils in the frozen, snow-covered earth of Antarctica. But paleontologists have done it! Learn more about fossils like *Cryolophosaurus* and *Antarctopelta* on page 104.

Muttaburrasaurus
(MUT-a-BURR-a-SORE-us):
"Muttaburra lizard,"
South America,
Early Cretaceous

Minmi
(MIN-mee):
Named for Minmi
Crossing,
Queensland, Australia,
Early Cretaceous

Trinisaura
(TRIH-nih-SORE-uh):
Named for geologist
Trinidad Diaz, Antarctica,
Late Cretaceous

SPOTLIGHT ON:
VICTORIA, AUSTRALIA

FOSSIL FINDS: *GALLEONOSAURUS, LEAELLYNASAURA*
WHEN: CRETACEOUS

AUSTRALIA

NEW ZEALAND

ANTARCTICA

Victoria was one of the coldest places in the world during the Cretaceous period. It was still not very cold compared with today's temperatures. But because it was close to the South Pole, it had long, dark winter nights. The dinosaurs that lived here were mostly small. They had to adapt to living with only a little sunlight for part of the year. Today, a lot of their fossils are found near Dinosaur Cove, a group of cliffs by the ocean in Victoria. This location is near the huge valley that formed between Australia and Antarctica during the Late Jurassic and Early Cretaceous.

VICTORIA

Dinosaurs that lived closer to the planet's poles, in places such as Australia and Antarctica, are called "polar dinosaurs." The weather here was colder than in other parts of the planet, but it was still mild compared to today.

GALLEONOSAURUS
(GAL-lee-on-oh-SORE-us)

MEANING:
"Galleon ship lizard"

PERIOD: Early Cretaceous

Scientists found five fossils of upper jawbones on the coast of Victoria. They came from a family of raccoon-size, two-legged plant-eaters. Each jaw was shaped like a type of ship called a galleon. So, the scientists named the dinosaur *Galleonosaurus*. It's closely related to ornithopods from the Patagonia region in South America. This makes scientists think that South America and Australia may have been connected by land during this time.

INDIAN OCEAN

Arafura Sea

PACIFIC OCEAN

Australia

Coral Sea

0 — 400 miles
0 — 400 kilometers

Great Australian Bight

Canberra, A.C.T.

Victoria

Dinosaur Cove

Map Key

⊛ Capital

○ Point of interest

□ Area of interest

LEAELLYNASAURA
(LEE-ELL-IN-a-SORE-a)

MEANING: "Leaellyn's lizard"

PERIOD: Early Cretaceous

This tiny two-legged dinosaur had a very long, very flexible tail. That's because the tail had more than 70 vertebrae. Some scientists think it was feathery. A feathered tail could have helped keep *Leaellynasaura* warm during the colder weather. *Leaellynasaura* also had large eyes. This was common for dinosaurs that lived this far south. They wouldn't see the sun for weeks at a time during some parts of the year. Larger eyes would have helped them see better in the dark.

UNSURE DINOSAURS

In 1984, scientists found a dinosaur jawbone and teeth in Victoria. But they could not find any other bones nearby. They named the dinosaur *Atlascopcosaurus*. But it also had another name: "nomen dubium." This is Latin for "unsure name." Most dinosaur finds are not whole skeletons. When only one or two bones are found, it is hard for scientists to figure out how long the dinosaur was, how much it weighed, or what it ate. Sometimes a dinosaur is named as a new genus or species, but experts who later review the finds decide that there is not enough evidence to say the fossils really are a new genus or species. Paleontologists then give these finds the name "nomen dubium" to show there is information missing. Since then, more *Atlascopcosaurus* fossils have been found, and it is no longer a nomen dubium.

SPOTLIGHT ON:
QUEENSLAND, AUSTRALIA

FOSSIL FINDS: *WINTONOTITAN, AUSTROLOVENATOR*
WHEN: CRETACEOUS

AUSTRALIA

NEW ZEALAND

ANTARCTICA

During the Early Cretaceous, half of Australia was flooded by shallow seas. The seas would rise and fall because of the moving continents. When sea levels were high, Australia had an inland body of water called the Eromanga Sea. As sea levels dropped, the Eromanga Sea dried up. It turned into a group of many rivers about 95 million years ago. Over millions of years, sediment from these rivers hardened into rock. Today, this rock makes up the Winton Formation in central Queensland. Lots of new fossils are found here every year.

QUEENSLAND OUTBACK, AUSTRALIA

WINTONOTITAN (WIN-ton-oh-TIE-tan)

MEANING: "Winton giant" PERIOD: Late Cretaceous

This four-legged titanosaur was about 50 feet (15 m) long. That's small for a titanosaur! Other titanosaurs could grow to lengths of 115 feet (35 m). *Wintonotitan* had longer front legs than other similar sauropods. Parts of a fossil were found in the 1970s. But it wasn't until 2004 and 2006 that more bones from the same species were found nearby. Finally, in 2009, the fossil was named *Wintonotitan*.

SILLY NAMES

Paleontologists are serious about dinosaurs, but they don't always give them serious names. Take *Diamantinasaurus matildae*: Australian scientists call this dinosaur "Matilda" after one of poet Andrew Barton Paterson's famous poems. Check out some of these other silly dinosaur names:

Colepiocephale: In Greek, this dinosaur's name means "knucklehead."
Gasosaurus: This dinosaur was named after gasoline! It was found during the construction of a gas company building.
Irritator: This species of spinosaur was named in recognition of how the scientists were feeling when they realized part of the fossil they were sold was a fake made by humans: irritated—meaning angry! (They removed the fake part and were able to study the real *Irritator* fossil.)

Arafura Sea

Coral Sea

INDIAN OCEAN

Queensland

A u s t r a l i a

Winton Formation

Great Australian Bight

PACIFIC OCEAN

⊛ Canberra, A.C.T.

Tasman Sea

Map Key

⊛ Capital

▢ Area of interest

▢ Winton Formation

0   400 miles
0   400 kilometers

AUSTRALOVENATOR
(OSS-trah-LOW-ven-ay-tor)

MEANING: "Southern hunter"

PERIOD: Late Cretaceous

Australovenator was a *megaraptor* found in 2006. Megaraptors were a group of large-clawed dinosaurs. They were fast predators. From head to tail, *Australovenator* was about 16 to 20 feet (5–6 m) long. That's a lot bigger than a *Velociraptor*! Theropods like *T. rex* had short arms, but *Australovenator*'s arms were longer. Each arm had three sharp claws to catch other animals for dinner.

Australovenator was given a nickname inspired by a famous Australian poet, Andrew Barton "Banjo" Paterson. The nickname for *Australovenator* is Banjo!

SPOTLIGHT ON:
ANTARCTICA

FOSSIL FINDS: *CRYOLOPHOSAURUS, ANTARCTOPELTA*
WHEN: JURASSIC AND CRETACEOUS

AUSTRALIA

NEW ZEALAND

ANTARCTICA

Today, Antarctica is very cold and icy. Average temperatures range from 14°F (-10°C) to minus 76°F (-60°C). But Antarctica wasn't always so cold—in fact, it didn't even have ice during the time of the dinosaurs! During the Early Jurassic, it was about 600 miles (965.6 km) north of where it is today. Then, it was a mild, warm forest. It was home to dinosaurs and other kinds of life. Today's cold weather and ice make it hard to hunt for fossils, but scientists still find them. In 2016, scientists uncovered more than a ton (about one metric ton) of marine life fossils, such as snails, clams, and cephalopods. They also found the fossils of Cretaceous dinosaurs.

ANTARCTICA

CRYOLOPHOSAURUS (CRY-oh-LOAF-oh-SORE-us)

MEANING: "Frozen crested lizard"

PERIOD: Early Jurassic

Found in 1991, *Cryolophosaurus* is Antarctica's most famous dinosaur. This Jurassic period predator is one of the oldest large meat-eating dinosaurs ever found. It was 20 feet (6 m) long. That was large for a theropod during this time. It's been nicknamed "Elvisaurus." This is because its curved crest looks like the hairstyle of the famous musician Elvis Presley!

EXTREME FOSSIL HUNTING: Antarctica

Antarctica is the coldest, driest, windiest place on Earth. That means it can be hard to travel on the continent. Ice and blizzards are dangerous. People can get frostbite, or freezing of their skin. The cold can also cause hypothermia, which is when the human body gets so cold it can't make enough heat. Scientists try to look for rock formations where fossils might be, but more than 97 percent of the ground is ice! They have to search for rocks that are aboveground and uncovered. But a snowstorm or windstorm could cover important finds at any moment.

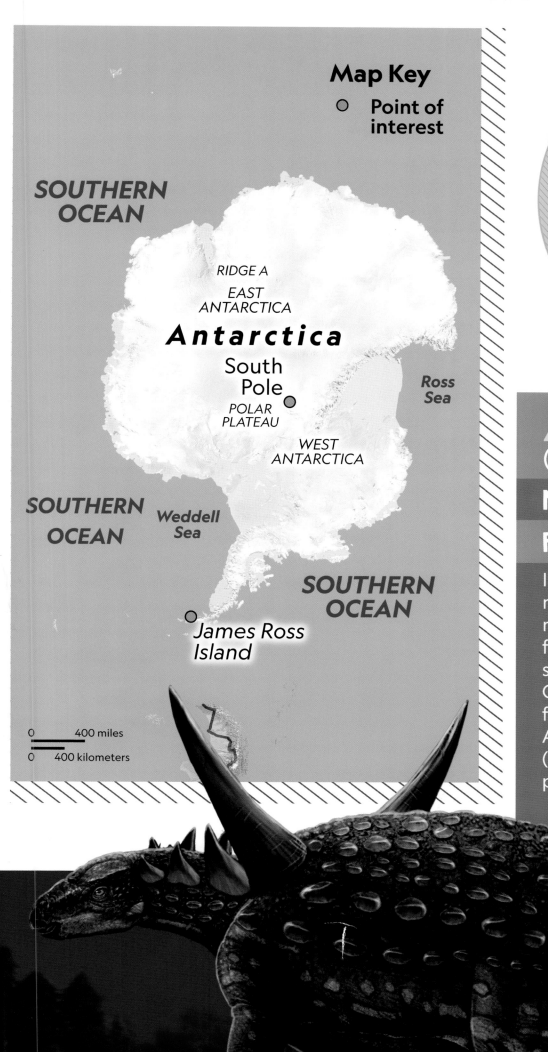

Map Key
○ Point of interest

SOUTHERN OCEAN

RIDGE A

EAST ANTARCTICA

Antarctica

South Pole

POLAR PLATEAU

WEST ANTARCTICA

Ross Sea

SOUTHERN OCEAN

Weddell Sea

SOUTHERN OCEAN

○ James Ross Island

0 —— 400 miles
0 —— 400 kilometers

As temperatures continue to rise because of global warming, ice in Antarctica will melt. It will uncover more rocks ... and the fossils inside those rocks. But it might also make it harder for humans and other animals around the planet to survive.

ANTARCTOPELTA
(ant-ARK-toe-PELT-uh)

MEANING: "Antarctic shield"

PERIOD: Late Cretaceous

In 1986, two geologists were hiking the northern part of James Ross Island, near the Antarctic Peninsula. They found a jawbone and some leaf-shaped teeth. The hikers, Eduardo Olivero and Roberto Scasso, were the first people to find a dinosaur fossil in Antarctica. The fossil was of a 20-foot (6-m)-long ankylosaur. It had thick plates, called osteoderms, that were like body armor. The fossil had been very damaged by the freezing temperatures. This meant it was hard to study, so the fossil wasn't named until 2006.

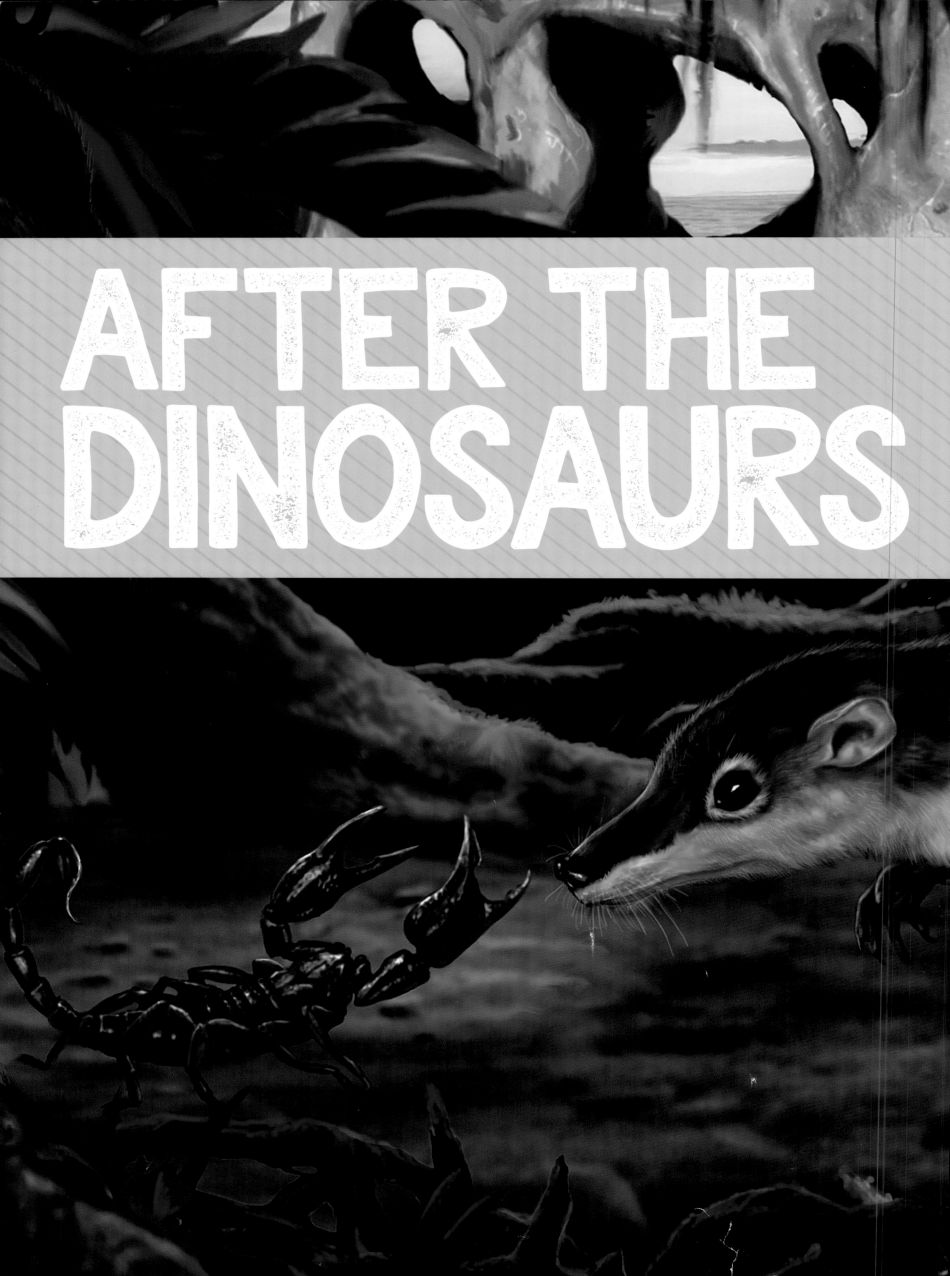

AFTER THE DINOSAURS

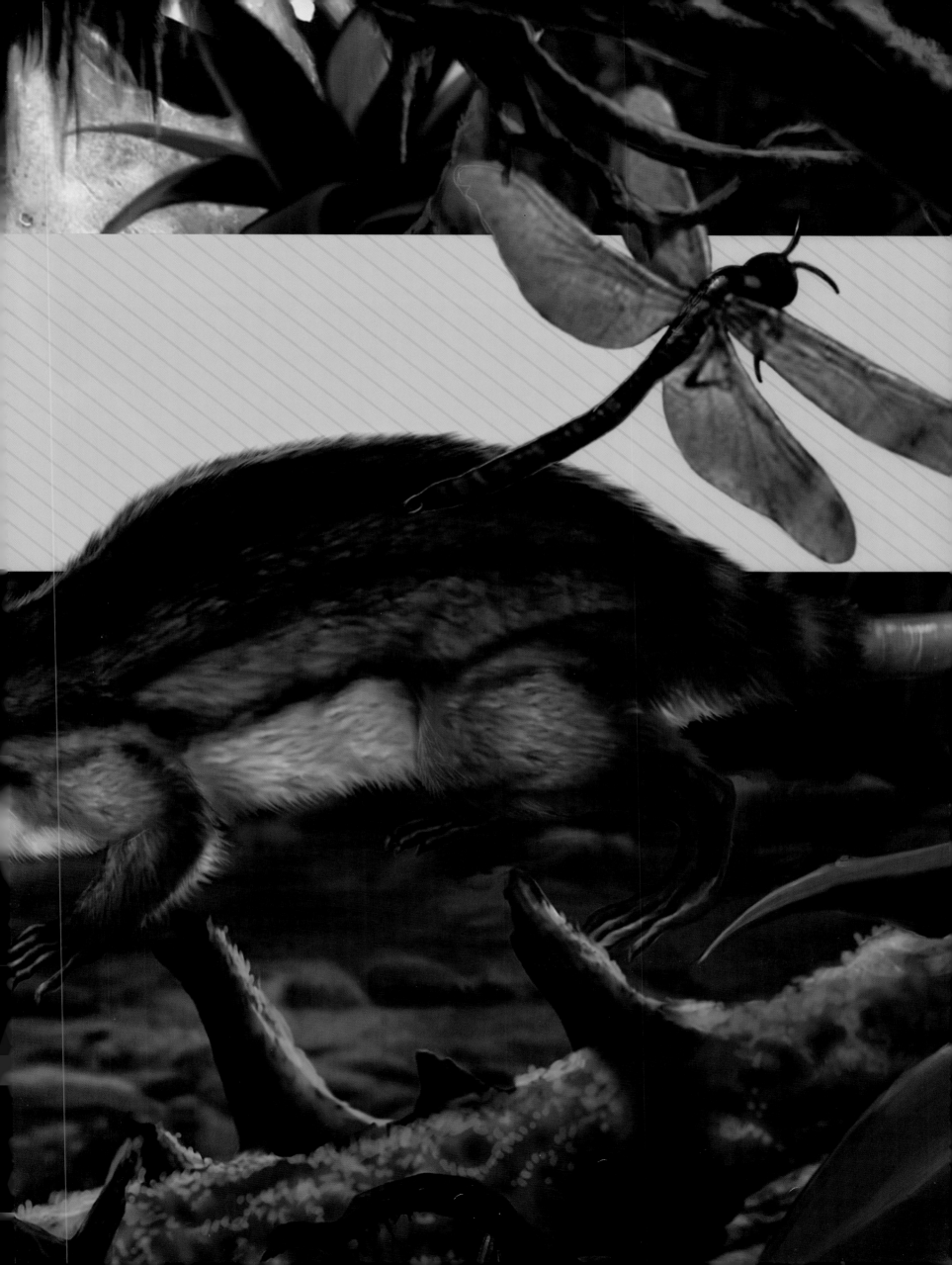

WHAT HAPPENED TO THE DINOSAURS?

About 70 to 75 percent of life on Earth died at the end of the Cretaceous period. A species becomes extinct when all members have died. That means there are no more remaining on the planet. A mass extinction occurs when huge numbers of entire species around the world die out over very short periods of time. That's what happened to the dinosaurs—sort of. Non-avian dinosaurs died, but many avian dinosaurs—whose descendants are now known as birds—survived! (Turn to page 112 to learn more about the bird-dinosaur connection.) Scientists have been trying to find out what happened to the non-avian dinosaurs for many years. They have come up with many ideas. Today, most scientists agree that the extinction was caused by an asteroid or comet that hit Earth.

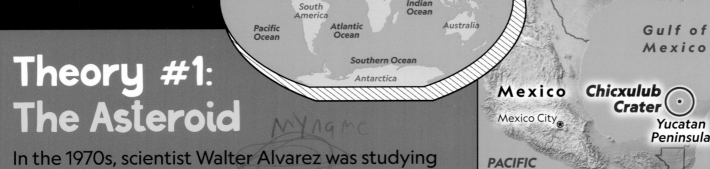

Theory #1: The Asteroid

In the 1970s, scientist Walter Alvarez was studying rocks in Italy. He found a layer of clay in between a layer of rock from the Cretaceous period and a layer of rock from the Paleogene period, the period after the Cretaceous. The clay layer was mixed with a chemical called iridium. Iridium is not common on Earth. But it is common in space.

In 1980, Alvarez and his father, Luis, shared an idea: A huge rock from space, called an asteroid, crashed as a meteor into Earth at the end of the Cretaceous period. This is what killed off the dinosaurs. But where had this meteor hit? In 1996, scientists began an exploration of a previously discovered six-mile (9.7-km)-wide crater. It was on the edge of Mexico's Yucatan Peninsula. The crater was mostly buried in the sea under almost 2,000 feet (610 m) of sediment. To study it, they used giant machines to drill into the rock. They named it the Chicxulub Crater, after a nearby village.

Now most scientists agree that about 66 million years ago, a meteor traveling at tens of thousands of miles an hour hit the Yucatan Peninsula. It caused mile-high tsunamis, huge earthquakes, volcanic eruptions, and massive wildfires. A dusty ash cloud covered Earth. It led to a period of darkness that might have lasted for months or even years. The darkness caused freezing temperatures and killed plants.

It was cold, and many of the plants that herbivores ate could not grow. Without enough food, the herbivores died. This meant that many carnivores now did not have enough herbivores to eat, so they died, too. Scientists don't know exactly what happened or how fast the dinosaurs died. But by about 10,000 years after the meteor hit, all non-avian dinosaurs were gone.

Could things have turned out differently for the dinosaurs? If the meteor had hit the ocean instead of land, the cloud of dust it shot into the air might have been less thick. Then sunlight could have peeked through the cloud, and the planet might have stayed warm ... and maybe dinosaurs would have lived.

The non-bird dinosaurs lived for about 175 million years. That's more than 500 times longer than *Homo sapiens* (modern humans) have lived!

OTHER EXTINCTION THEORIES

Most scientists agree that dinosaurs went extinct because of the meteor that struck Mexico's Yucatan Peninsula. But some think other events may have made dinosaurs go extinct. Other scientists think they may have gone extinct for a combination of reasons.

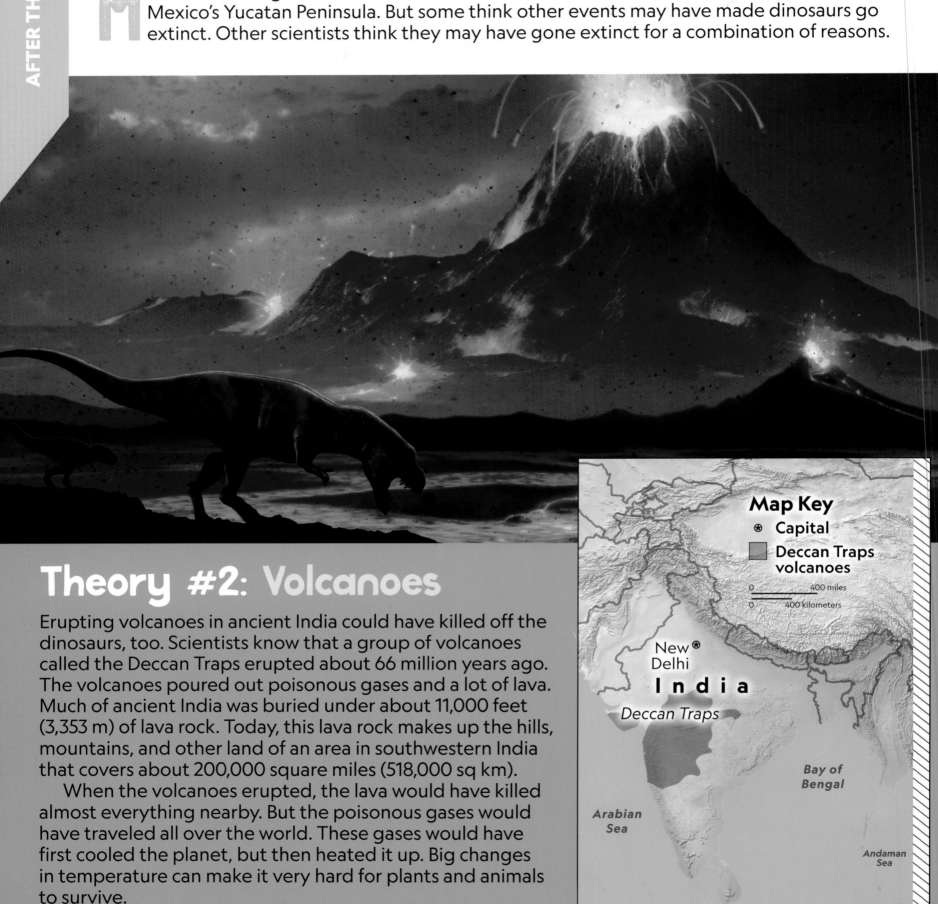

Theory #2: Volcanoes

Erupting volcanoes in ancient India could have killed off the dinosaurs, too. Scientists know that a group of volcanoes called the Deccan Traps erupted about 66 million years ago. The volcanoes poured out poisonous gases and a lot of lava. Much of ancient India was buried under about 11,000 feet (3,353 m) of lava rock. Today, this lava rock makes up the hills, mountains, and other land of an area in southwestern India that covers about 200,000 square miles (518,000 sq km).

When the volcanoes erupted, the lava would have killed almost everything nearby. But the poisonous gases would have traveled all over the world. These gases would have first cooled the planet, but then heated it up. Big changes in temperature can make it very hard for plants and animals to survive.

Scientists have found more information by studying the age of the lava rocks. They know the Deccan Traps erupted more than once—before and after the meteor hit. This makes some scientists think the Deccan Traps were the biggest cause of the dinosaur extinction.

Map Key

⊛ Capital

▢ Deccan Traps volcanoes

0   400 miles

0   400 kilometers

New ⊛ Delhi

I n d i a

Deccan Traps

Arabian Sea

Bay of Bengal

Andaman Sea

INDIAN OCEAN

Theory #3: Slow Climate Change

Most dinosaurs went extinct 66 million years ago, but some other animals (and avian dinosaurs) survived. How is that possible? Some scientists think there wasn't one huge event that caused a mass extinction. Instead, there might have been several smaller events.

The largest extinction event in history was the Permian-Triassic extinction 252 million years ago. It happened when volcanoes erupted in Siberia. Changes in climate came after these eruptions. Some scientists think the Cretaceous extinction happened more like this: Several things happened that changed the climate from the warm and mild Mesozoic era to the cooler Cenozoic era. That cool climate slowly killed ocean life and plant life. Then it eventually killed the non-avian dinosaurs.

AGE OF MAMMALS

You could say that the mass extinction of the dinosaurs was very unlucky. But it was lucky for us! The Age of Reptiles was followed by the Age of Mammals. That includes us humans! Some small furry mammals survived the extinction. With no dinosaurs around to eat them, they could become the main creatures on Earth.

WOOLLY MAMMOTHS ROAMED EARTH FIVE MILLION TO 4,000 YEARS AGO.

DINO DESCENDANTS

Do dinosaurs rule the planet today? Not exactly—but they do rule the skies. Birds are dinosaurs. Yes, even the tiniest hummingbird! The birds that fly—and flightless birds that walk the planet today—all evolved from maniraptoran dinosaurs. Maniraptoran dinosaurs were a group of theropods that included *Velociraptor* and *Oviraptor*.

The mass extinction killed the non-avian dinosaurs 66 million years ago. But some avian dinosaurs lived on.

Of all the avian dinosaurs, scientists believe the ones that lived on the ground and ate seeds survived. Those avian dinosaurs evolved into the bird species we know today. The avian dinosaurs that lived in trees became extinct. That's because forests on Earth would have been destroyed after the asteroid struck the Yucatan Peninsula.

Today, there are more than 10,000 living bird species around the world.

NOTHRONYCHUS

DEFINITELY ANCESTORS

What do birds and non-avian dinosaurs have in common? More than you think! They both lay and hatch from eggs. They both have scales (birds have scales on their feet). Lastly, their skeletons are very similar.

CROW TALONS

YI QI

In 2014, scientists used chickens to try to learn how *Tyrannosaurus rex* might have walked. To do this, they put fake dinosaur tails on the chickens!

PREHISTORIC BIRDS

Some of the earliest birds have been described as half bird, half *Velociraptor*. Some of them couldn't even fly. Scientists study these kinds of fossils to try to learn more about how modern birds came to be. The Jurassic period *Archaeopteryx* (p. 75) remains one of the most famous dinosaur fossils ever found. It's the oldest known bird on the family tree. But in the past few decades, more and more avian dinosaur fossils have been found. This means that scientists have lots to study.

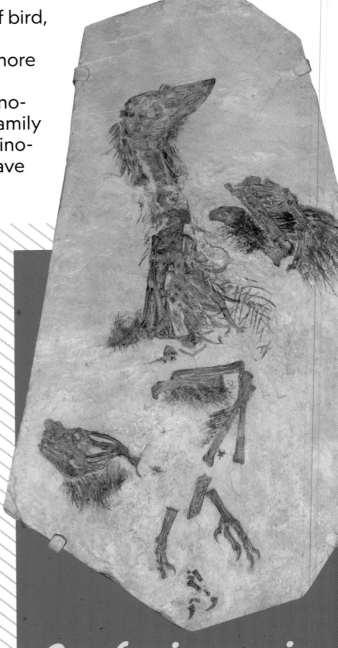

Tsidiiyazhi
(SID-ee-YAH-zhee)
Meaning: "Little morning bird"
Type: Theropod
Period: Paleocene
Location: Nacimiento Formation, New Mexico, U.S.A.

Found on Navajo land in 2017, this sparrow-size bird lived after the Cretaceous extinction. It had a fourth toe, which makes scientists think it lived in trees. The toe could bend backward to grab branches.

Confuciusornis
(kon-FEW-shus-OR-niss)
Meaning: "Confucius bird"
Type: Theropod
Period: Early Cretaceous
Location: Yixian Formation, China

Hundreds of whole fossils of this small, crow-size bird have been found. Its toothless beak was different from *Archaeopteryx*'s toothfilled mouth. This makes it one of the earliest known birds to have a beak like modern birds. It may have eaten fish. *Confuciusornis* had a pair of long ribbon-like tail feathers.

Crossvallia

(kross-VAH-lee-uh)
Meaning: Named for the Cross Valley
Type: Sphenisciformes
Period: Early Paleocene
Location: South Island, New Zealand

This giant penguin was as tall as an adult human! It stood more than five feet (1.6 m) tall and could weigh between 155 and 175 pounds (70–80 kg). *Crossvallia* was first found in the early 2000s. A second species was found in 2019 by a fossil hunter named Leigh Love. Scientists think these penguins grew so large because there weren't many animals around to hunt them. Dinosaurs and large marine reptiles had gone extinct just before these ancient penguins lived.

Jinguofortis

(JEEN-gwo-FOR-tis)
Meaning: "Female warrior"
Type: Theropod
Period: Early Cretaceous
Location: Hebei, China

This crow-size bird was announced by scientists in 2018. It had a 27-inch (70-cm) wingspan. And it had a unique shoulder bone that makes scientists think it may have flown differently from how birds fly today. This early bird also had a tooth-filled jaw instead of a beak. Its tail was shorter than its long-tailed relatives like *Archaeopteryx*. The short tail is called a pygostyle. *Jinguofortis* is one of the earliest fossils to have one.

Vegavis

(vay-GAH-vis)
Meaning: "Vega bird"
Type: Theropod
Period: Late Cretaceous
Location: Vega Island, Antarctica

This extinct bird looked a lot like a modern duck—and may have even sounded like one! Scientists found this fossil in 1992. But it wasn't until 2013 that they noticed its syrinx, or voice box. A voice box is a body part that lets animals make sound through their mouths. Before this, the syrinx of a dinosaur had never been found—avian or non-avian. This tells scientists that dinosaurs may have grown voice boxes late in the Cretaceous period. Before that, they may have made sounds in other ways.

DINO DICTIONARY

A

NAME & PRONUNCIATION	MEANING	GEOLOGIC TIME	WHERE FOUND	LENGTH	GROUP
ACHILLOBATOR ah-kill-oh-BATE-or	"Achilles hero"	Late Cretaceous	Asia	16 feet (5 m)	Maniraptorans
AEGYPTOSAURUS ee-JIP-tuh-SORE-us	"Egyptian lizard"	Early to Late Cretaceous	Africa	50 feet (15 m)	Sauropods
AFROVENATOR af-ro-VEN-ah-tor	"African hunter"	Middle Jurassic	Africa	50 feet (15 m)	Sauropods
AGILISAURUS ah-JIL-ih-SORE-us	"Fast lizard"	Late Jurassic	Asia	3.5 to 4 feet (1.–1.7 m)	Ornithischians
AJKACERATOPS AHJ-ka-SEHR-uh-tops	"Horn face from Ajka"	Late Cretaceous	Europe	3 feet (1 m)	Ceratopsians
ALBERTOSAURUS al-BERT-oh-SORE-us	"Alberta lizard"	Late Cretaceous	North America	25 feet (7.6 m)	Tyrannosaurs
ALLOSAURUS AL-oh-SORE-us	"Strange lizard"	Middle to Late Jurassic	Asia, Europe, North America	28 feet (8.5 m)	Allosaurs
ALVAREZSAURUS al-var-rez-SORE-us	"Alvarez's lizard"	Late Cretaceous	South America	6 feet (2 m)	Maniraptorans
ANKYLOSAURUS AN-kee-loh-SORE-us	"Stiff lizard"	Late Cretaceous	North America	25 to 35 feet (7.6–10.6 m)	Ankylosaurs
ANTARCTOPELTA ant-ARK-toe-PELT-uh	"Antarctic shield"	Late Cretaceous	Antarctica	20 feet (6 m)	Ankylosaurs
ANTARCTOSAURUS ant-ARK-toe-SORE-us	"Non-northern lizard"	Late Cretaceous	South America	60 to 100 feet (19–30 m)	Sauropods
APATOSAURUS uh-PAT-uh-SORE-us	"Tricky lizard"	Late Jurassic	North America	70 feet (21 m)	Sauropods
ARCHAEOPTERYX ARK-ee-OP-turr-icks	"Ancient wing"	Late Jurassic	Europe	1.6 feet (0.5 m)	Theropods
ARGENTINOSAURUS AR-gen-TEEN-oh-SORE-us	"Argentina lizard"	Late Cretaceous	South America	121 feet (37 m)	Sauropods
ATACAMATITAN AT-ah-COM-uh-TIE-tin	"Giant from the Atacama Desert"	Late Cretaceous	South America	Unknown	Sauropods
ATLASCOPCOSAURUS AT-lass-COP-ko-SORE-us	"Atlas Copco lizard"	Early Cretaceous	Australia	6.5 to 10 feet (2–3 m)	Ornithopods
AUSTRALOVENATOR OSS-trah-LOW-ven-ay-tor	"Southern hunter"	Late Cretaceous	Australia	16 to 20 feet (5–6 m)	Theropods
AUSTROPOSEIDON OSS-troh-poh-SYE-don	"Southern Poseidon [Greek god]"	Late Cretaceous	South America	82 feet (25 m)	Sauropods
AUSTROSAURUS OSS-trah-SORE-us	"Southern lizard"	Early Cretaceous	Australia	50 feet (15 m)	Sauropods

B

NAME & PRONUNCIATION	MEANING	GEOLOGIC TIME	WHERE FOUND	LENGTH	GROUP
BAGUALOSAURUS bag-WALL-oh-SORE-us	"Strongly built lizard"	Late Triassic	South America	8 feet (2.5 m)	Sauropod-omorphs
BALAUR BONDOC BAL-or BON-doc	"Stocky dragon"	Late Cretaceous	Europe	7 feet (2 m)	Maniraptorans
BARAPASAURUS BAH-rap-oh-SORE-us	"Big leg lizard"	Early Jurassic	Asia	60 feet (20 m)	Sauropods

NAME & PRONUNCIATION	MEANING	GEOLOGIC TIME	WHERE FOUND	LENGTH	GROUP
BARYONYX bah-ree-ON-icks	"Heavy claw"	Early Cretaceous	Europe	28 feet (8.5 m)	Theropods
BEIPIAOSAURUS BAY-pyow-SORE-us	"Beipiao lizard"	Early Cretaceous	Asia	7.3 feet (2.2 m)	Maniraptorans
BRACHIOSAURUS BRAK-ee-oh-SORE-us	"Arm lizard"	Late Jurassic	Africa, Europe, North America	80 to 85 feet (24–26 m)	Sauropods

C

NAME & PRONUNCIATION	MEANING	GEOLOGIC TIME	WHERE FOUND	LENGTH	GROUP
CAMPTOSAURUS KAMP-toe-SORE-us	"Bent lizard"	Late Jurassic	Europe	23 feet (7 m)	Ornithopods
CAUDIPTERYX CAW-dip-TEHR-iks	"Tail feather"	Early Cretaceous	Asia	3 feet (1 m)	Maniraptorans
CENTROSAURUS SEN-troh-SORE-us	"Sharp pointed lizard"	Late Cretaceous	North America	20 feet (6 m)	Ceratopsians
CERATOSAURUS SEHR-uh-toe-SORE-us	"Horned lizard"	Late Jurassic to Early Cretaceous	Africa, North America	20 feet (6 m)	Theropods
CHASMOSAURUS KAZ-mo-SORE-us	"Chasm lizard"	Late Cretaceous	North America	16 feet (5 m)	Ceratopsians
CHENANISAURUS che-NAN-ih-SORE-us	"Chenan lizard"	Late Cretaceous	Africa	23 to 26 feet (7–8 m)	Theropods
CHILESAURUS CHEE-lay-SORE-us	"Chile lizard"	Late Jurassic	South America	11 feet (3.4 m)	Ornithischians or theropods
CHINDESAURUS CHIN-dee-SORE-us	"Chinde lizard"	Late Triassic	North America	6.5 feet (2 m)	Theropods
CHIROSTENOTES kie-ROH-sten-OH-teez	"Narrow-handed"	Late Cretaceous	North America	9.5 feet (2.9 m)	Maniraptorans
CHUBUTISAURUS choo-boot-i-SORE-us	"Chubut [Province] lizard"	Early Cretaceous	South America	75 feet (23 m)	Sauropods
COAHUILACERATOPS koh-WHEE-lah-SEHR-uh-tops	"Horn face from Coahuila"	Late Cretaceous	North America	22 feet (7 m)	Ceratopsians
COELOPHYSIS SEE-low-FY-sis	"Hollow form"	Late Triassic to Early Jurassic	Africa, North America	6.5 feet (2 m)	Theropods
COLORADISAURUS KO-lo-RAHD-ih-SORE-us	"Los Colorados lizard"	Late Triassic	South America	10 to 13 feet (3–4 m)	Sauropodomorphs
COMPSOGNATHUS COMP-sog-NAY-thus	"Elegant jaw"	Late Jurassic to Early Cretaceous	Europe	3 feet (0.9 m)	Theropods
CONFUCIUSORNIS kon-FEW-shus-OR-niss	"Confucius bird"	Early Cretaceous	Asia	20 inches (50.8 cm)	Theropods
CORYTHOSAURUS koh-RITH-oh-SORE-us	"Corinthian helmet lizard"	Late Cretaceous	North America	30 feet (9 m)	Hadrosaurs
CROSSVALLIA kross-vah-lee-uh	Named for the Cross Valley	Early Paleocene	New Zealand	5 feet (1.6 m)	Spenisciformes
CRYOLOPHOSAURUS CRY-oh-LOAF-oh-SORE-us	"Frozen crested lizard"	Early Jurassic	Antarctica	20 feet (6 m)	Theropods

D

NAME & PRONUNCIATION	MEANING	GEOLOGIC TIME	WHERE FOUND	LENGTH	GROUP
DACENTRURUS DAH-sen-TROO-russ	"Pointed tail"	Late Jurassic	Europe	20 feet (6 m)	Stegosaurs
DELTADROMEUS DEL-tah-DROH-mee-us	"Delta runner"	Late Cretaceous	Africa	26 feet (8 m)	Theropods

NAME & PRONUNCIATION	MEANING	GEOLOGIC TIME	WHERE FOUND	LENGTH	GROUP
DIAMANTINASAURUS DIE-uh-mun-TEE-nuh-SORE-us	"Diamantina [River] lizard"	Late Cretaceous	Australia	50 feet (15 m)	Sauropods
DIPLODOCUS DIP-low-DOCK-us	"Double beam"	Late Jurassic	North America	90 feet (27 m)	Sauropods
DREADNOUGHTUS dred-NAUT-us	"Oak lizard"	Late Jurassic	North America	10 to 12 feet (3–3.5 m)	Ornithopods

E

NAME & PRONUNCIATION	MEANING	GEOLOGIC TIME	WHERE FOUND	LENGTH	GROUP
EDMONTONIA ed-mon-TONE-ee-ah	"Of Edmonton"	Late Cretaceous	North America	20 to 23 feet (6–7 m)	Ankylosaurs
EORAPTOR EE-oh-RAP-tor	"Early thief"	Late Triassic	South America	5 feet (1.5 m)	Saurischians
EUROPASAURUS yoo-ROH-pah-SORE-us	"Europe lizard"	Late Jurassic	Europe	20 feet (6.2 m)	Sauropods

F

NAME & PRONUNCIATION	MEANING	GEOLOGIC TIME	WHERE FOUND	LENGTH	GROUP
FUKUIRAPTOR foo-koo-ee-RAP-tor	"Fukui thief"	Early Cretaceous	Asia	14 to 20 feet (4.2–6 m)	Theropods
FUKUISAURUS foo-koo-ee-SORE-us	"Fukui lizard"	Early Cretaceous	Asia	16 feet (5 m)	Ornithopods
FULGUROTHERIUM FOOL-gur-oh-THEE-ree-um	"Lightning beast"	Late Cretaceous	Australia	6.5 feet (2 m)	Ornithopods

G

NAME & PRONUNCIATION	MEANING	GEOLOGIC TIME	WHERE FOUND	LENGTH	GROUP
GALLEONOSAURUS GAL-lee-on-oh-SORE-us	"Galleon ship lizard"	Early Cretaceous	Australia	Unknown	Ornithopods
GALLIMIMUS gal-lee-MEEM-us	"Chicken copy"	Late Cretaceous	Asia	17 feet (5.5 m)	Ornithomimosaurs
GARGOYLEOSAURUS gahr-GOY-lee-oh-SORE-us	"Gargoyle lizard"	Late Jurassic	North America	10 feet (3 m)	Ankylosaurs
GASOSAURUS GAS-oh-SORE-us	"Gas lizard"	Middle Jurassic	Asia	12 feet (3.5 m)	Theropods
GIGANOTOSAURUS gig-an-OH-toe-SORE-us	"Giant southern lizard"	Late Cretaceous	South America	43 feet (13 m)	Theropods
GIRAFFATITAN ji-RAF-a-TIE-tan	"Giant giraffe"	Late Jurassic	Africa	75 feet (23 m)	Sauropods
GLACIALISAURUS GLAY-shull-ih-SORE-us	"Icy lizard"	Early Jurassic	Antarctica	20 to 25 feet (6–7.5 m)	Sauropodomorphs
GRACILICERATOPS GRAS-i-li-SEHR-uh-tops	"Thin horned face"	Late Cretaceous	Asia	3 to 5 feet (0.8–1.5 m)	Ceratopsians
GUAIBASAURUS GWIE-bah-SORE-us	"[Rio] Guaiba lizard"	Late Triassic	South America	5 to 10 feet (1.5–2.9 m)	Sauropodomorphs

H

NAME & PRONUNCIATION	MEANING	GEOLOGIC TIME	WHERE FOUND	LENGTH	GROUP
HERRERASAURUS herr-ray-rah-SORE-us	"Herrera's lizard"	Late Triassic	South America	16.5 feet (5 m)	Theropods
HETERODONTOSAURUS HET-er-oh-DAHNT-oh-SORE-us	"Different teeth lizard"	Early Jurassic	Africa	4 feet (1.2 m)	Ornithopods
HUNGAROSAURUS HUN-gah-roh-SORE-us	"Hungary lizard"	Late Cretaceous	Europe	13 feet (4 m)	Ankylosaurs
HYLAEOSAURUS HIGH-lee-oh-SORE-us	"Woodland lizard"	Early Cretaceous	Europe	20 feet (6 m)	Ankylosaurs
HYPSILOPHODON hip-sih-LOH-foh-don	"High-ridge tooth"	Early Cretaceous	Europe	7.5 feet (2.3 m)	Sauropods

I & J

NAME & PRONUNCIATION	MEANING	GEOLOGIC TIME	WHERE FOUND	LENGTH	GROUP
IGUANODON ig-WHA-no-don	"Iguana tooth"	Early Cretaceous	Europe	33 feet (10 m)	Ornithopods
INDOSUCHUS IN-doh-SOOK-us	"Indian crocodile"	Late Cretaceous	Asia	20 feet (6 m)	Theropods
IRRITATOR IRR-it-ate-or	"Irritator"	Early Cretaceous	South America	25.5 feet (8 m)	Theropods
JINGUOFORTIS JEEN-gwo-FOR-tis	"Female warrior"	Early Cretaceous	Asia	Wingspan of 27 inches (70 cm)	Theropods
JOBARIA joh-BAR-ee-uh	"Jobar [mythical animal]"	Middle Jurassic	Africa	70 feet (21 m)	Sauropods
JURAVENATOR ju-RAH-ve-NAY-tor	"Hunter from Jura"	Late Jurassic	Europe	1.3 feet (0.4 m)	Tyrannosaurs

K

NAME & PRONUNCIATION	MEANING	GEOLOGIC TIME	WHERE FOUND	LENGTH	GROUP
KENTROSAURUS KEN-troh-SORE-us	"Spiky lizard"	Late Jurassic	Africa	17 feet (5 m)	Stegosaurs
KHAAN kahn	"Ruler"	Late Cretaceous	Asia	4 feet (1.2 m)	Maniraptorans

L

NAME & PRONUNCIATION	MEANING	GEOLOGIC TIME	WHERE FOUND	LENGTH	GROUP
LAQUINTASAURA lah-KWEEN-tuh-SORE-uh	"Lizard of La Quinta"	Early Jurassic	South America	3 feet (1 m)	Ornithischian
LEAELLYNASAURA LEE-ELL-IN-a-SORE-a	"Leaellyn's lizard"	Early Cretaceous	Australia	6.5 to 10 feet (2–3 m)	Ornithopods
LEDUMAHADI LAY-do-mah-HA-dee	"Giant thunderclap"	Late Cretaceous	Africa	6 feet (1.8 m)	Ceratopsians
LILIENSTERNUS lil-ee-en-SHTERN-us	Named for Count Hugo Rühle von Lilienstern	Late Triassic	Europe	16 feet (5 m)	Theropods
LURDUSAURUS LUR-doh-SORE-us	"Heavy lizard"	Early Cretaceous	Africa	27 to 30 feet (8.4–9 m)	Ornithopods

M

NAME & PRONUNCIATION	MEANING	GEOLOGIC TIME	WHERE FOUND	LENGTH	GROUP
MACROCOLLUM MACK-row-COLL-um	"Long neck"	Late Triassic	South America	11 feet (3 m)	Sauropod-omorphs
MANSOURASAURUS man-SOUR-uh-SORE-us	"Mansoura lizard"	Late Cretaceous	Africa	33 feet (10 m)	Titanosaurs
MASSOSPONDYLUS MASS-oh-SPON-dih-lus	"Huge vertebrae"	Early Jurassic	Africa	13 feet (4 m)	Sauropod-omorphs
MAXAKALISAURUS MAX-a-KAL-ee-SORE-us	"Maxakali [tribe of Brazil] lizard"	Late Cretaceous	South America	43 feet (13 m)	Theropods
MEGALOSAURUS MEG-ah-low-SORE-us	"Big lizard"	Middle Jurassic	Europe	27 feet (8.5 m)	Theropods
MELANOROSAURUS MEL-an-OR-oh-SORE-us	"Black [Mountain] lizard"	Late Triassic to Early Jurassic	Africa	40 feet (12 m)	Sauropod-omorphs
MICRORAPTOR MIKE-row-RAP-tor	"Tiny thief"	Early Cretaceous	Asia	2 to 4 feet (0.7–1.2 m)	Theropods
MINMI MIN-mee	Named for Minmi Crossing, Queensland	Early Cretaceous	Australia	6.6 feet (2 m)	Ankylosaurs
MUSSAURUS moos-SORE-us	"Mouse lizard"	Late Triassic	South America	10 feet (3 m)	Sauropod-omorphs
MUTTABURRASAURUS MUT-a-BURR-a-SORE-us	"Muttaburra lizard"	Early Cretaceous	Europe	24 feet (7 m)	Ornithopods

N

NAME & PRONUNCIATION	MEANING	GEOLOGIC TIME	WHERE FOUND	LENGTH	GROUP
NEOVENATOR NEE-oh-ven-AY-tor	"New hunter"	Early Cretaceous	Europe	26 feet (8 m)	Theropods
NIGERSAURUS NYE-jer-SORE-us	"Niger lizard"	Early Cretaceous	Africa	30 feet (9 m)	Sauropods
NQWEBASAURUS n-qu-WEB-ah-SORE-us	"Nqweba lizard"	Early Cretaceous	Africa	2.5 feet (0.8 m)	Theropods
NYASASAURUS ny-AS-ah-SORE-us	"Lizard of Lake Nyasa"	Middle Triassic	Africa	10 feet (3 m)	Archosaurs

O

NAME & PRONUNCIATION	MEANING	GEOLOGIC TIME	WHERE FOUND	LENGTH	GROUP
OMEISAURUS OH-may-SORE-us	"Omei lizard"	Middle Jurassic	Asia	68 feet (20 m)	Sauropods
ORNITHOLESTES OR-nith-oh-LES-teez	"Bird robber"	Late Jurassic	North America	6.5 feet (2 m)	Theropods
OTHNIELIA OTH-ni-EH-lee-a	Named for Othniel [Marsh]"	Late Jurassic	North America	4.6 feet (1.4 m)	Ornithischians
OVIRAPTOR OH-vih-RAP-tor	"Egg thief"	Late Cretaceous	Asia	5 feet (1.5 m)	Theropods

P

NAME & PRONUNCIATION	MEANING	GEOLOGIC TIME	WHERE FOUND	LENGTH	GROUP
PARALITITAN pa-RAL-ih-tie-tuhn	"Tidal giant"	Late Cretaceous	Africa	Up to 100 feet (30 m)	Sauropods
PARASAUROLOPHUS PAR-a-sore-OL-off-us	"Like Saurolophus"	Late Cretaceous	North America	7 feet (2 m)	Ornithopods

NAME & PRONUNCIATION	MEANING	GEOLOGIC TIME	WHERE FOUND	LENGTH	GROUP
PATAGOTITAN PAH-tah-go-TIE-tan	"Giant from Patagonia"	Early Cretaceous	South America	120 feet (36 m)	Sauropods
PELECANIMIMUS pel-e-kan-i-MIM-us	"Pelican copy"	Early Cretaceous	Europe	6.5 feet (2 m)	Ornithomimosaurs
PHUWIANGOSAURUS POO-WEE-ong-oh-SORE-us	"Phu Wiang lizard"	Early Cretaceous	Asia	50 feet (15 m)	Sauropods
PHUWIANGVENATOR POO-WEE-ong-ven-AY-tor	"Phu Wiang hunter"	Early Cretaceous	Asia	18 feet (5.5 m)	Theropods
PLATEOSAURUS plat-EE-oh-SORE-us	"Flat lizard"	Late Triassic	Europe	16 to 33 feet (5–10 m)	Sauropods
POLACANTHUS pol-a-KAN-thus	"Many spines"	Early to Late Cretaceous	Europe	15 feet (4.6 m)	Ankylosaurs
PROCOMPSOGNATHUS PRO-COMP-sog-NAY-thus	"Before the elegant jaw"	Late Triassic	Europe	3.8 feet (1.2 m)	Theropods
PROTOCERATOPS PRO-toh-SEHR-uh-tops	"First horned face"	Late Cretaceous	Asia	6 feet (1.8 m)	Ceratopsians
PSITTACOSAURUS SIT-ah-coh-SORE-us	"Parrot lizard"	Early Cretaceous	Asia	5.6 feet (2 m)	Ceratopsians

Q

NAME & PRONUNCIATION	MEANING	GEOLOGIC TIME	WHERE FOUND	LENGTH	GROUP
QANTASSAURUS KWON-tuh-SORE-us	Named for Qantas Airlines	Early Cretaceous	Australia	6 feet (1.8 m)	Ornithopods

R

NAME & PRONUNCIATION	MEANING	GEOLOGIC TIME	WHERE FOUND	LENGTH	GROUP
RAJASAURUS RAH-zha-SORE-us	"King lizard"	Late Cretaceous	Asia	30 feet (9 m)	Theropods
REBBACHISAURUS reh-BASH-ih-SORE-us	"Rebbach lizard"	Late Cretaceous	Africa	68 feet (20 m)	Sauropods
RHABDODON RAB-doh-don	"Rod tooth"	Late Cretaceous	Europe	13 feet (4 m)	Ornithopods
RHOETOSAURUS REET-oh-SORE-us	"Rhoetan lizard"	Late Jurassic	Australia	40 feet (12 m)	Sauropods
RIOJASAURUS ree-OH-hah-SORE-us	"Lizard from La Rioja"	Late Triassic	South America	36 feet (11 m)	Sauropodomorphs
RUGOPS ROO-gops	"Wrinkle face"	Late Cretaceous	Africa	27 feet (8 m)	Theropods

S

NAME & PRONUNCIATION	MEANING	GEOLOGIC TIME	WHERE FOUND	LENGTH	GROUP
SAICHANIA sie-CHAN-ee-a	"Beautiful"	Late Cretaceous	Asia	23 feet (7 m)	Ankylosaurs
SALTASAURUS SALT-ah-SORE-us	"Salta lizard"	Late Cretaceous	South America	40 feet (12 m)	Sauropods
SCELIDOSAURUS skel-EYE-doh-SORE-us	"Limb lizard"	Early Jurassic	Europe	13 feet (4 m)	Ornithischians

NAME & PRONUNCIATION	MEANING	GEOLOGIC TIME	WHERE FOUND	LENGTH	GROUP
SCIURUMIMUS ski-UR-u-MEE-mus	"Squirrel copy"	Late Jurassic	Europe	Unknown	Theropods
SINOSAUROPTERYX SINE-oh-SORE-op-TEHR-iks	"Chinese lizard wing"	Early Cretaceous	Asia	3.3 feet (1 m)	Theropods
SINRAPTOR sine-RAP-tor	"Chinese thief"	Late Jurassic	Asia	26 feet (8 m)	Theropods
SIRINDHORNA SEER-en-TORN-uh	Named for Princess Maha Chakri Sirindhorn	Early Cretaceous	Asia	20 feet (6 m)	Ornithopods
SPINOSAURUS SPINE-oh-SORE-us	"Spine lizard"	Early to Late Cretaceous	Africa	50 feet (15 m)	Theropods
STRUTHIOMIMUS STROO-thee-oh-MEEM-us	"Ostrich copy"	Late Cretaceous	North America	14 feet (4.3 m)	Ornithomimosaurs
STRUTHIOSAURUS STROO-thee-oh-SORE-us	"Ostrich lizard"	Late Cretaceous	Europe	7 feet (2 m)	Ankylosaurs

T

NAME & PRONUNCIATION	MEANING	GEOLOGIC TIME	WHERE FOUND	LENGTH	GROUP
TACHIRAPTOR TAW-chee-RAP-tor	"Thief of Táchira"	Early to Late Jurassic	South America	5 feet (1.5 m)	Theropods
TALARURUS TAL-a-RUR-us	"Wicker tail"	Late Cretaceous	Asia	20 feet (6 m)	Ankylosaurs
TAWA ta-wa	"Big hollow"	Late Triassic	North America	13 feet (4 m)	Theropods
TELMATOSAURUS tel-ma-toh-SORE-us	"Swamp lizard"	Late Cretaceous	Europe	16 feet (5 m)	Ornithopods
THECODONTOSAURUS THEEK-o-DON-toh-SORE-us	"Socket-toothed lizard"	Late Triassic	Europe	7 feet (2.1 m)	Sauropodomorphs
TRICERATOPS try-SEHR-uh-tops	"Three horned face"	Late Cretaceous	North America	30 feet (8 m)	Ceratopsians
TRINISAURA TRIH-nih-SORE-uh	Named for geologist Trinidad Diaz	Late Cretaceous	Antarctica	4.9 feet (1.5 m)	Ornithopods
TSIDIIYAZHI SID-ee-YAH-zhee	"Little morning bird"	Paleocene	North America	Unknown	Theropods
TSINTAOSAURUS sin-tau-SORE-us	"Qingdao lizard"	Late Cretaceous	Asia	33 feet (10 m)	Ornithopods
TYRANNOSAURUS ti-RAN-oh-SORE-us	"Tyrant lizard"	Late Cretaceous	North America	40 feet (12 m)	Theropods

U & V

NAME & PRONUNCIATION	MEANING	GEOLOGIC TIME	WHERE FOUND	LENGTH	GROUP
UNENLAGIA OON-en-LAHG-ee-ah	"Half-bird"	Late Cretaceous	South America	7.5 feet (2.2 m)	Maniraptorans
ULUGHBEGSAURUS oo-LOOG-bek-SAW-rus	Named for a 15th-century astronomer and mathematician	Late Cretaceous	Asia	25 feet (7.5 m)	Theropods
VEGAVIS vay-GAH-vis	"Vega bird"	Late Cretaceous	Antarctica	2 feet (0.6 m)	Theropods
VELAFRONS VEHL-uh-fronz	"Sailed forehead"	Late Cretaceous	North America	25 feet (8 m)	Hadrosaurs

NAME & PRONUNCIATION	MEANING	GEOLOGIC TIME	WHERE FOUND	LENGTH	GROUP
VELOCIRAPTOR vel-OSS-ih-RAP-tor	"Quick thief"	Late Cretaceous	Asia	6.5 feet (2 m)	Maniraptorans
VULCANODON vul-KAN-oh-DON	"Vulcan [Roman god] tooth"	Early Jurassic	Africa	20 feet (6.1 m)	Sauropods

W

NAME & PRONUNCIATION	MEANING	GEOLOGIC TIME	WHERE FOUND	LENGTH	GROUP
WINTONOTITAN WIN-ton-oh-TIE-tan	"Winton giant"	Late Cretaceous	Australia	50 feet (15 m)	Sauropods

Z

NAME & PRONUNCIATION	MEANING	GEOLOGIC TIME	WHERE FOUND	LENGTH	GROUP
ZUNICERATOPS ZOO-nee-SEHR-uh-tops	"Zuni horned face"	Late Cretaceous	North America	12 feet (3.7 m)	Ceratopsians

Glossary

ALLOSAUR – a type of carnivorous dinosaur, usually with a long, narrow skull and small arms that ended in three-fingered hands

AMMONITE – a mollusk in a spiral shell that lived in the Mesozoic era

ANKYLOSAUR – a type of four-legged, armored dinosaur that was likely a herbivore

AVIAN DINOSAUR – a bird.

BADLANDS – an area of land where few plants grow, and wind and water have worn away the soft rocks into different shapes

CAMBRIAN PERIOD – the earliest period of the Paleozoic era, 541 to 485 million years ago, when almost all large spineless animal groups and fish appeared on Earth

CARBONIFEROUS PERIOD – the fifth period of the Paleozoic era, 359 to 299 million years ago. In North America, the Carboniferous is split into the Mississippian and Pennsylvanian periods. During this time, huge swamps and surrounding forests were found in Europe and North America.

CARNIVORE – a meat-eater. Nearly all dinosaur meat-eaters had sharp teeth with jagged edges like a steak knife to help slice through meat.

CENOZOIC ERA – a unit of geologic time when mammals, birds, flowering plants, and grasses quickly evolved. This is the geologic era Earth is in now.

CERATOPSIAN – a type of four-legged dinosaur whose large head had horns, a beak, and a bony frill

COELUROSAUR – the name for a group of theropod dinosaurs very similar to birds. However, bird-like dinosaurs outside this group have also been found.

CONIFER – a group of many kinds of evergreen trees. Their leaves are usually needle-shaped. These types of trees do not lose their leaves in the fall.

CREST – a grouping of feathers, fur, or skin on the top of an animal's head

CRETACEOUS PERIOD – the third and last period of the Mesozoic era, 145 to 66 million years ago. Most dinosaurs became extinct at the end of this period.

DEVONIAN PERIOD – the fourth period of the Paleozoic era, 419 to 359 million years ago. Ferns, insects, and amphibians ruled the land and the first ammonites appeared in seas.

DINOSAUR – an extinct group of carnivorous or herbivorous reptiles that lived during the Mesozoic era

ERA – a long and distinct time in history

EVOLVE – to change over time

EXCAVATE – to remove or make hollow by digging out material

EXTINCTION – an end to one or more forms of life

FOSSIL – a preserved body part, track, or trace of an ancient animal, insect, or plant

GEOLOGIC TIME – the eras and periods of Earth's history

GONDWANA – a large continent, formed of today's South America, Africa, Antarctica, and Australia, that was believed to have existed in Earth's Southern Hemisphere during the end of the Paleozoic Era

HABITAT – a certain environment of plants and animals

HERBIVORE – a plant-eater. Most dinosaurs were herbivores. Their teeth were designed to grind or cut plants, and their stomachs were built to digest plants.

HETERODONTOSAUR – a type of very early ornithischian dinosaur

ICHTHYOSAUR – a type of large marine reptile, similar in appearance to a dolphin, that is now extinct

JURASSIC PERIOD – the second period of the Mesozoic era, 201 to 145 million years ago, when dinosaurs lived and birds first appeared on Earth

LAURASIA – a large landmass made up of North America, Europe, and Asia that was believed to have existed in the Northern Hemisphere during the end of the Paleozoic era

MAMMAL – warm-blooded animals with spines, including humans and other animals that are covered with hair and make milk to feed their young

MANIRAPTORAN – a type of carnivorous dinosaur that ran quickly on two legs and had a large claw on each foot and hand

MEGALOSAUR – a huge carnivorous dinosaur that lived during the Jurassic and Early Cretaceous

MESOZOIC ERA – the era of geologic time that includes the Triassic, Jurassic, and Cretaceous periods. During this time, flying reptiles, birds, and flowering plants appeared on Earth.

NEOGENE PERIOD – a period of geologic time from 23 million years ago to 2.6 million years ago when the Earth became cooler and drier. This period is in the Cenozoic era.

OMNIVORE – an animal that eats both plants and other animals

ORDOVICIAN PERIOD – the second period of the Paleozoic era of geologic time, 485 to 444 million years ago, when fish first appeared on Earth

ORNITHOMIMOSAUR – type of two-legged dinosaur that ran quickly on two legs and often had no teeth

ORNITHOPODS – type of herbivorous dinosaur that likely walked on two legs—although some used the toes of their front limbs to walk on all fours

PACHYCEPHALOSAURS – a type of two-legged dinosaur with a thick skull and a domed or flat head

PALEOCENE PERIOD – the earliest part (66 to 56 million years ago) of the Paleogene period (66 to 23 million years ago), in the Cenozoic era of geologic time, when mammals evolved from small and simple forms into many kinds of animals

PALEONTOLOGIST – a scientist who studies extinct organisms and their environments

PALEOZOIC ERA – the era of Earth's history when vertebrates and land plants first appeared on Earth

PANGAEA – a land area that once connected the Northern and Southern Hemispheres 235 to 200 million years ago

PERIOD – a unit of geologic time

PERMIAN PERIOD – the sixth period of the Paleozoic era, 299 to 252 million years ago, when most animals and plants became extinct and reptiles began to rule the land

PREDATOR – an animal that hunts for food

PTEROSAUR – an extinct flying reptile of the Mesozoic era

PYGOSTYLE – a bone found in modern birds at the end of the spine. It supports the tail.

QUATERNARY PERIOD – a period of geologic time from 2.6 million years ago to the present, when mammoths and modern humans appeared on Earth. This period is in the Cenozoic era.

SAUROPOD – a type of large four-legged herbivore with a long neck and tail and a small head

SAUROPODOMORPHS – the group that includes sauropods and their earlier relatives

SEDIMENT – tiny pieces of material such as rock, plants, or animals

SILURIAN PERIOD – the third period in the Paleozoic era, 444 to 419 million years ago, when fish evolved into many forms

SPHENISCIFORMES – an order of flightless marine birds that includes penguins

SUPERCONTINENT – a large continent made of more than one of today's continents that has since broken apart

STEGOSAUR – a type of four-legged herbivore with defensive plates along its back

THEROPOD – a type of carnivorous dinosaur that likely moved on two legs

THYREOPHORANS – a group of four-legged dinosaurs with defensive armor or plates

TRIASSIC PERIOD – the first period of the Mesozoic era, 252 to 201 million years ago, when dinosaurs and mammals first appeared on Earth

TYRANNOSAUR – a large carnivore that moved on two legs and had a powerful jaw and small arms that ended in two fingers

VERTEBRATE – refers to animals that have backbones or spinal columns

A note for parents and teachers: For more information on dinosaurs, you can check out these resources with your young readers.

Resources

BOOKS

Brusatte, Steve. *The Age of Dinosaurs.* Quill Tree Books: New York, 2021.

Brusatte, Steve. *Day of the Dinosaurs: Step Into a Spectacular Prehistoric World.* Wide-Eyed Editions: London, 2016.

DK Eyewitness Books: Fossil. New York: DK Publishing, Inc., 2017.

Lessem, Don. *Ultimate Dinopedia.* Washington, D.C.: National Geographic, 2017.

Nargi, Lela. *Absolute Expert: Dinosaurs.* Washington, D.C.: National Geographic, 2018.

National Geographic Kids Dino Records. Washington, D.C.: National Geographic, 2017.

Sampson, Scott. *You Can Be a Paleontologist!* Washington, D.C.: National Geographic, 2017.

Stein, Megan. *What Was the Age of Dinosaurs?,* Penguin Workshop, 2017.

Waters, Kate. *Curious About Fossils.* New York: Smithsonian, 2016.

MOVIES AND TV SHOWS

National Geographic:
Bizarre Dinosaurs
Dinosaur Hunters: Secrets of the Gobi Desert
I Love Dinosaurs
Really Wild Animals: Dinosaurs and Other Creature Features
Sky Monsters
T. rex Autopsy

BBC
Allosaurus: A Walking With Dinosaurs Special
Chased by Dinosaurs
Planet Dinosaur
Walking With Dinosaurs (show and movie)

Discovery
Clash of the Dinosaurs
Dinosaur Planet
Dinosaurs: Inside and Out

APPS

BBC Earth Walking With Dinosaurs: Inside Their World

Britannica Kids: Dinosaurs

Dinosaurs: The American Museum of Natural History Collection

National Geographic March of the Dinosaurs

National Geographic Ultimate Dinopedia: The Most Complete Dinosaur Reference Ever

PBS Kids Dinosaur Train A to Z

Smithsonian's Prehistoric Pals: It's *Tyrannosaurus Rex*